Dad's Home Cooking: Traditional Recipes for Preparing Healthy Family Meals

ISBN-10: 1-480-16500-X (paperback)

ISBN-13: 978-1-480-16500-7 (paperback)

First edition, 2012

Copy Editor: Lisa Gordanier
Proofer: Heather Miller and Mark Berens
Cover and Book Design: Jessica Merrill
Illustrations: Justin van Duersen
Editorial and Project Management: Girl Friday Productions
Front and back cover photograph: Richard Owen

DAD'S
HOME COOKING

Traditional Recipes for Preparing Healthy Family Meals

By R. W. Owen

Table of Contents

About This Book

This book is for everyone, from those just starting in the kitchen to those experienced cooks who are looking for something new to prepare. You'll find day-to-day recipes, as well as menu items that I often prepare for holidays and special occasions. Most are easy to make with common, readily available ingredients. This is not a general purpose, all-inclusive cookbook, which you should also have on hand (my favorite is *The New Good Housekeeping Cookbook*, published in 1986), so I've excluded the basics, such as how to scramble eggs or boil vegetables.

You will need some simple utensils to prepare the foods in this book. If you lack what is needed, I recommend buying what you need on sale or buy used items. Check out the thrift/junk stores and garage/estate sales in your area. (My definition of a garage sale: "An opportunity to trade junk with your neighbors.") Also check out used household items in local classifieds or on Craigslist. Limit your secondhand purchases to stainless steel, cast iron, copper, and glass. Avoid buying rusty/chipped utensils and used aluminum, coated aluminum pots and pans, and plastic items.

I have included two sections at the end of this book not typically found in cookbooks: "Seasoning Your Food: Herbs, Spices, and Aromatics" (page 207) that discusses how to grow and cook with common herbs and spices, as well as providing information on the aromatics that enhance our cooking: onions, leeks, shallots, garlic, and horseradish. "What Else to Keep on Hand" (page 217) is a handy list to help you stock your home with essential food items.

I hope these recipes interest and even inspire you—and I trust that you will enjoy them as much as I have. It is my pleasure to share them with you.

Bon Appétit!

R. W. Owen

Kenmore, Washington

List of Recipes

Appetizers

Salads and Soups

Main Dishes

Desserts

Breakfast Dishes

Breads

Sauces and Condiments

Introduction

My first memory of cooking was at four or five years old. My grandmother, mom, and aunt would fix an enormous noon meal for the grain-threshing crew who harvested wheat with binders, stationary threshing machines, and horse-drawn wagons in the hot August weather. My job was to peel a large basket of potatoes. After feeding the crew, the cooks and kids would eat what remained. It was an experience that made me realize the work that went in to feeding ourselves and our families.

I grew up on a farm near Hollister, Idaho—a small town of fifty people, about halfway between Jackpot, Nevada, and Twin Falls, Idaho. Hollister had two general stores selling limited food items, mainly canned and dry goods, soda pop, candy, bread, processed meats, and bananas. My family could drive to these stores and buy a few of the food items we needed, or ask my grandfather to pick up something when he drove to Hollister to get the mail every day except Sunday. Once you had selected what you needed, the store owner would write down the items you chose and expect you to pay your bill with cash or check by the end of the month. If you failed to pay, then no more credit.

By the time I started elementary school in 1950, we were, for the most part, raising a good portion of the food we ate. We had a large garden and chickens, and my grandparents, who lived nearby, provided milk from their cow. We slaughtered our own beef and pork. Hunting in the fall added deer and pheasant meat to our table; occasionally, we went fishing on summer weekends for trout, perch, and blue gill.

I attended Hollister School built in 1912 for grades 1 to 12. (When I attended, it served only grades 1 to 6.) Today it is the oldest continuously operating school building in the state of Idaho, listed in the National Register of Historic Places. For two weeks at the start of school in the fall and for two weeks at the end of the school term, we took our lunches (bologna sandwiches, which we never got at home) and something sweet. For the rest of the school year we ate hot lunches, which everyone had to buy in order for the program to be financially feasible. (The PTA sponsored Saturday night dances with live music in Hollister to raise funds for the program.) School lunches were cooked using government surplus food with some vegetables grown by farmers and canned by our mothers. The fruit was all canned; I remember only once in six years being served a fresh half apple. There was no milk available as the milk processing plants in Twin Falls were too far for delivery. The meals were served on Navy surplus metal trays with tin cups filled with water, which was treated with bleach since the tap water was not chlorinated.

Junior high and high school were joined in one complex in Filer, a small town east of Twin Falls. The hot lunches there were a step above elementary school and we were served milk. In seventh and eighth grades, students could volunteer to wash dishes in the cafeteria kitchen for a free meal, so I took advantage of that opportunity to pocket my lunch money. School was let out for two weeks in October for potato harvest and I would pick spuds with my mother to earn extra money. By 1958, this October break was eliminated as potato harvesting machines were making handpicking obsolete. (1958 was also when we got a party line telephone and a half-day, one-station TV.)

Twin Falls was quite a drive from our farm, so we only made the trip once a week to haul eggs to market and buy supplies and food items that we needed. The grocery stores carried only produce that was in season, so for most of the year there wasn't much selection. When Fourth of July came, we couldn't wait to taste the first trucked-in California watermelon of the summer. We picked cherries, peaches, and apples that were grown in the Snake River Canyon and my mom canned what we didn't eat fresh.

The closest restaurants were in Twin Falls, so eating out was not an option. (I was in eighth grade before I ate in a restaurant other than a drive-in or lunch counter.) Needless to say, I grew up in a family that fed itself with home-cooked meals; a concept that I carried with me, for the most part, into my adult life.

I have been cooking since I was eleven years old. Even though I had developed some campfire cooking skills in Boy Scouts, my culinary abilities flourished when I joined the local 4-H cooking club. My sister, who is thirteen months younger than me, had been actively involved in 4-H, so I knew a bit about 4-H exhibits and cooking demonstrations at the Twin Falls County Fair. Taking bread to exhibit at the fair was my introduction to making bread, though I was somewhat familiar with the process from watching my mother make bread and dinner rolls for our family.

My father did no serious day-to-day cooking. He did like to make fruit cakes and clothesline taffy for Christmas. (Clothesline taffy is pulled taffy that you drape over the clothesline in the cold winter so that it freezes hard and becomes brittle. It can then be cracked into serving pieces.) He made his pancakes for breakfast every day and always had my mother fix cooked carrots for dinner.

My parents thought it was important for my sister and I to learn as many skills as possible, though, so they taught us how to farm, raise a garden, take care of animals, cook, and preserve foods by canning, freezing, and pickling. We also learned basic carpentry and how to safely handle firearms.

By the time I got out of high school, I could also weld and do blacksmithing work and basic mechanics, mostly learned during four years of vocational agriculture in high school. In addition to helping on the farm, I worked with my dad and sometimes my uncle building houses, where I learned about wiring and plumbing, as well as how to build concrete forms, place and finish concrete, frame structures, build cabinets, plaster walls, lay brick, and block and shingle a roof.

Despite the fact that all these skills could have been used to make a living, I chose to travel four hundred and fifty miles to go to the University of Idaho and take on five years of study in architecture. I spent almost all of those years living at FarmHouse Fraternity, and for two years, I served as Business Manager, in charge of planning meals with our hired cook and buying all the food for the forty men in the house. This group was friendly, but they never hesitated to complain about the meals—even though we ate far better, and at less cost, than the dorms and other fraternities and sororities on campus. Both cooks I worked with were quirky and somewhat difficult to manage, which gave me an appreciation of the restaurant industry and the difficulties involved in hiring and keeping a good, dependable, talented staff.

I remember one Mother's Day dinner when, inexplicably, the cook did not show up for work. This was a yearly event—a formal, sit-down meal honoring our mothers. It was the most important dinner of the year, and I had no cook to prepare it. There was no way we could cancel the meal, so I cooked with help from some other fraternity brothers. Dinner was served, with none of the mothers ever wiser. When the cook arrived the next morning, she was amazed that a group of guys had managed to cook and serve the dinner without her. She never pulled that trick again.

I spent one summer and fall of my last year in college working part-time in a pizza parlor/beer hall. This short stint was my only experience working in the fast-food industry, but it was good experience for my adult life, and I worked my tail off. On a busy night, my kitchen partner and I would assemble, bake, and sell two hundred pizzas!

After college I went to work as an architect and I only had to cook to feed myself. Within a few years, I was married with children, but still not doing the major day-to-day meal preparation. That changed when I found myself, for the most part, responsible for raising and feeding three kids alone. This meant three meals a day, seven days a week. I learned how to fix a large Sunday dinner so we could have quick leftover meals one or two days during the week. We occasionally ate out on Fridays—a real treat. I also used and developed many recipes that were quick and easy to make. We never ate out of boxes, except for cold cereal once in a while. I remember buying and serving TV dinners one evening, and the kids refusing to eat them. I always encouraged my kids to try new things, and they learned to eat a good variety of foods.

Because I could cook, I didn't panic when the kids came home saying they needed to bring a dish to the end-of-the-year soccer picnic or a batch of cookies to class. Arriving at the picnic with homemade potato salad (which got raves from everyone) was better than coming with a box of donuts or a bag of potato chips.

I also honed my skills by cooking for friends. We would take turns hosting Saturday-night dinner. So, about once a month, I was able to either prepare the meal at my house or bring a dish to other homes. Sometimes, I was asked to cook a dish I had never made before; this way, I was able to try new menu items and, if they were well received and fairly easy to make, add them to my regular repertoire. I must admit that I made a few dishes I didn't like and one that I tried to feed to the family was so bad that we tossed it. I also cooked holiday meals for my family and close friends, with guests contributing a side dish. It is a real job to fix an elaborate holiday meal, but I always enjoyed doing it.

After the kids were gone, I started making my own beer and wine and returned to growing vegetables, after many years of not doing so. Garden growing turned into pickle making, and the adventure continues.

Appetizers

Appetizers are the way to get your meal off to a good start. If everyone likes your first course, chances are they will eagerly anticipate the main dinner. These dishes can also stand alone as party noshes.

Appetizers should be easy, simple, and quick to make. For a few of the more complicated recipes in this chapter, I've included information on how to prepare them ahead. If you don't have time to make an appetizer, then simply serve a unique cheese with crackers. There are also many prepared frozen goodies that can be heated and served in a pinch, such as pizza rolls and petite quiches. Many are costly, so buy them on sale and freeze until they are needed. Fruit or vegetable trays (with or without dip) also make good appetizers.

Bacon-Wrapped Prunes

Serves 4. Prep time: 25 minutes.

These warm, salty-sweet bites are delicious and always popular. Guests always ask, "What's in the middle?"

1 pound thin-sliced bacon (about 25 slices)

1 package (7 to 8 ounces) pitted dried prunes (about 25 pieces)

1. Preheat oven to 350 degrees F.

2. Wrap each prune in a whole strip of bacon and secure with a toothpick.

3. Place wrapped prunes on a rimmed baking sheet (to contain bacon grease) and bake for 15 minutes or until bacon is well cooked, turning if necessary to brown all sides. Remove from oven, drain fat, and serve warm.

BBQ Shrimp

Serves 4. Prep time: 15 minutes, plus marinating time (2 hours to overnight).

This recipe uses bamboo, wooden, or stainless steel skewers. To prevent bamboo or wooden skewers from catching fire, presoak in water for 30 minutes. Cook on an outside grill or use your oven's broiler.

24 large peeled, deveined, and cooked shrimp (about 2 pounds), tails removed

½ cup olive oil

2 tablespoons hot sauce

1 tablespoon ketchup

1 teaspoon Worcestershire sauce

2 cloves garlic, crushed

¼ cup fresh-squeezed lemon juice (about 1 large lemon)

½ teaspoon cayenne pepper

½ teaspoon fresh thyme leaves

½ teaspoon fresh rosemary leaves

½ teaspoon fresh oregano leaves

1 teaspoon freshly ground black pepper

1 teaspoon iodized salt

1. Wash shrimp, drain, and place in a large sealable plastic bag.

2. Add all remaining ingredients to bag and mix well. Seal bag and place in refrigerator for 2 hours or overnight.

3. Preheat broiler or grill to medium heat (350 degrees F).

4. Slide shrimp onto skewers.

5. Discard marinade.

6. Grill shrimp briefly on each side until they are heated and serve immediately.

Cocktail Meatballs in Dill Sauce

Makes 60 meatballs (about 15 servings). Prep time: Meatballs, 1 hour; Dill sauce, 30 minutes.

I suggest making the meatballs ahead and freezing them. You may make the dill sauce and finish the dish up to 1 hour before serving and keep it warm in a chafing dish. This recipe requires a deep fryer. If you do not have a fryer, place the meatballs on a rimmed baking sheet and bake in the oven at 350 degrees F until done. (The balls will be flat on the bottom but they are just as delicious.)

Meatballs:

⅓ cup long-grain white rice

1 cup water

1½ pounds ground beef

½ pound ground unseasoned pork

1 cup 2 percent milk

½ cup fresh whole wheat bread crumbs

2 green onions, chopped

1 tablespoon butter, melted

1 teaspoon fish sauce

½ teaspoon ground ginger

½ teaspoon ground allspice

½ teaspoon freshly ground white pepper

About 3 cups refined peanut oil for deep frying

Dill sauce:

½ cup finely chopped onion

1 garlic clove, minced

4 tablespoons (½ stick) butter

¼ cup all-purpose flour

1 (14.5 ounce) can beef broth

½ cup white wine

1 cup sour cream

1 teaspoon dried dill weed

1 teaspoon fish sauce

1 teaspoon freshly ground white pepper

Meatballs:

1. In a small saucepan, add rice and water and cook over medium heat until fluffy, following package instructions. Set aside.

2. While rice is cooking, place ground beef and ground pork in a food processor with the metal blade and process for about 2 minutes, stopping to scrape the bowl occasionally, until meat is finely and evenly ground.

3. When rice is done, add it and remaining ingredients (except for peanut oil) to the food processor and mix for 30 seconds, until well combined.

4. Add at least 2 inches of oil to an electric deep fryer and preheat to 350 degrees F. (or use a deep saucepan over medium-high heat).

5. Shape meat mixture into balls about 1 inch in diameter.

6. Lower fryer basket into oil and use a slotted spoon to carefully lower meatballs individually into oil until 6 balls are immersed. (Depending on the size of your fryer, adjust quantity if necessary so that balls do not touch.)

7. Cook meatballs for 3 minutes or until they are nicely browned and done in the middle. (Check by cutting one in half.) Remove fryer basket with cooked meatballs from oil and drain on paper towels.

8. Cook and drain remaining meatballs in batches until all are cooked. Remember to allow a minute or so for oil to reheat to 350 degrees before adding next batch.

9. Let meatballs cool briefly then refrigerate to cool completely or freeze in plastic freezer bags.

Dill sauce:

1. In a large skillet over medium heat, sauté onions and garlic in butter for 1 minute.

2. Stir in flour and continue cooking until mixture is bubbly.

3. Gradually add beef broth and wine, whisking to combine.

4. Bring to a boil then reduce heat to medium low, stirring continuously until mixture thickens.

5. Reduce heat to low (if mixture is too hot, the sour cream will separate) and stir in sour cream, dill, fish sauce, and pepper.

To assemble:

1. Add meatballs to dill sauce and heat gently over low heat for 15 minutes.

2. To serve, transfer to chafing dish.

Corn Dog Bites

Makes 18 pieces. Prep time: about 30 minutes.

Serve with your favorite mustard or use my homemade Mustard (page 174). This recipe requires a deep fryer.

Hot dogs:

About 3 cups refined peanut oil or enough to provide 2 inches of oil in electric deep fat fryer
6 hot dogs, each cut into 3 pieces (18 pieces total)

Batter:

½ cup yellow cornmeal

1½ cups all-purpose flour

4 teaspoons baking powder

1 tablespoon sugar

1 teaspoon iodized salt

1 cup 2 percent milk

3 large eggs, beaten

1. Add oil to an electric deep fryer (or use a deep saucepan over medium-high heat) until it is at least 2 inches deep. Preheat the oil to 350 degrees F.

2. Mix all batter ingredients in a bowl.

3. Lower frying basket into hot oil.

4. Dip hot dog pieces one at a time into batter and use a slotted spoon to carefully lower pieces individually into hot oil until 6 are immersed. (Depending on the size of your fryer, adjust quantity if necessary so pieces do not touch.)

5. Cook for about 3 minutes or until golden brown, stirring and separating the pieces with a fork if necessary.

6. Remove fry basket from oil and drain the corn dog bites on paper towels. Keep warm in oven.

7. Repeat until all pieces are cooked. Remember to allow a minute or so for the oil to reheat to 350 degrees before adding the next batch. Serve warm.

Deviled Eggs

Makes 24 egg halves. Prep time: about 30 minutes.

The filling will firm up a bit and the flavor will improve if made a day ahead. I generally make these for Easter dinner.

12 large eggs

½ cup mayonnaise

¼ cup prepared yellow mustard

½ teaspoon iodized salt

½ teaspoon freshly ground black pepper

1 teaspoon hot sauce (I prefer Tabasco)

Paprika, for garnish

Fresh chives or parsley, for garnish

1. In a large pan, cover eggs with water and a lid and bring to a boil. Turn off heat and let eggs cook with the pan still on the burner for 12 minutes. Pour off hot water and add cold water and ice to cool the eggs thoroughly.

2. When eggs are cold, peel them under water and then dry and slice in half lengthwise, using a knife or crinkle-cut garnish knife for more decorative edges.

3. Remove egg yolks, placing egg white halves on the serving platter and yolks in a small mixing bowl.

4. Add remaining ingredients (except garnish items) to egg yolks and mix thoroughly with a fork until all the yolk is mashed and mixed with the other ingredients.

5. Spoon egg yolk mixture into egg white cavities until all of the mixture is used.

6. Wash chives, cut into 1-inch pieces and insert 3 pieces into each egg or wash and insert a sprig of parsley.

7. Sprinkle a dash of paprika on each egg.

8. Cover and refrigerate until ready to serve.

Jalapeño Poppers

Makes 25 poppers. Prep time: 30 minutes to make stuffing; 30 minutes to stuff and grill.

You can make stuffing ahead of serving time and refrigerate it. These are HOT. If you want a milder popper, use milder chilies, such as sweet banana. (Use only the bottom 2 inches of the sweet banana pepper.) You will need a pepper roaster designed for use on an outdoor grill; it has holes that hold the peppers in an upright position. Most of these hold 18 peppers at a time, so you'll need to do 2 batches to make this entire recipe. If you do not have a pepper roaster, you can make 50 poppers by cutting the peppers in half longitudinally, stuffing the cavity with the filling, and setting the pepper halves on the grill.

1½ cups chorizo sausage (about 2 stuffed large sausages, casings removed)

½ cup finely chopped onion

1 cup shredded sharp cheddar cheese

½ cup cream cheese (preferably "light")

25 jalapeño peppers

1. Brown chorizo in a small skillet over medium heat. Drain and cool. Crumble it into small pieces. 2. In a small bowl, mix together chorizo, onion, and cheeses. This can be done ahead of time and refrigerated for up to 5 days.

2. Wash jalapeño peppers and cut off stem ends; remove seeds and veins inside the pepper. Use gloves and avoid breathing the vapors until you know how you react to preparing the peppers. (I do mine under water in a bowl, using a potato peeler to remove the insides.)

3. Place peppers in the holes of the pepper roaster.

4. Stuff peppers with filling by rolling filling into short "ropes" and inserting into pepper. Pack the filling and leave the top heaped up.

5. Place pepper roaster on a hot grill (about 400 degrees F); cook for about 15 minutes or until peppers are brown on the bottom and filling is bubbly.

6. Let cool briefly before serving.

Onion Bloom

Makes 4 onions (8 servings). Prep time: 15 minutes the first day; the next day, 30 minutes.

This delicious appetizer can also be served as a side dish. This recipe requires a deep fryer.

4 large sweet onions, such as Walla Walla, Ailsa Craig, or Vidalia

3 to 4 cups refined peanut oil, for frying

1 cup all-purpose flour

1 teaspoon iodized salt

1 teaspoon freshly ground white pepper

1 teaspoon paprika

1 cup buttermilk

Day before serving:

1. Peel onions and slice ½ inch off top of the onion.

2. Trim root end so onion will sit without falling over.

3. Cut onion into 8 sections by making a star pattern: With onion sitting on its root end, make a down cut to within ½ inch of the bottom through the onion's center. Turn onion 90 degrees and make second down cut also through onion's center, at a right angle to the first cut. Then make 2 more cuts at 45 degrees to the first cuts to make 8 sections of the onion.

4. Next, cut the wide, outer onion layers into 2 sections by carefully cutting each of them (starting from the outside and cutting in through several layers) in half.

5. Submerge onions in ice water and refrigerate overnight; onion layers will open up.

30 minutes before serving:

1. Preheat oven to 200 degrees F.

2. Remove onions from ice water and drain well.

3. Preheat oil in deep fryer to 350 degrees F.

4. In a small bowl, mix flour, salt, pepper, and paprika.

5. Sprinkle flour mixture on one onion to coat all layers, spreading them apart if necessary. (This assumes your deep fryer will handle only one onion at a time. If you are using a larger fryer, you can do more at the same time.)

6. Dip onion in buttermilk to coat all layers, and again sprinkle with flour mixture.

7. Shake off excess batter. Lower onion carefully into hot oil using a slotted spoon. Fry for 5 to 7 minutes until onion is golden brown, turning if necessary.

8. Drain well by turning onion upside down on paper towels and keep warm in the oven.

9. Repeat until all onions are fried. Remember to allow a minute or so for oil to reheat to 350 degrees before adding the next onion.

10. Serve immediately with Dill Weed Dip (page 16), Horseradish Sauce (page 173) or Ranch Dressing (page 36).

Salmon Pâté

Serves 12. Prep time: 10 minutes, plus chilling time (2 hours to overnight).

This pâté can be made a day ahead of time and refrigerated to better blend the flavor. Serve on crackers or use in sandwiches.

1 pound cold or hot smoked salmon, skin and bones removed

1 (8 ounce) package cream cheese, softened

¼ cup finely chopped green onion

1 tablespoon fresh lemon juice

¼ teaspoon dried dill weed

½ teaspoon ground black pepper

2 tablespoons capers, drained

1. Place all ingredients except capers into a blender or food processor fitted with the steel blade.

2. Process until mixture is smooth.

3. Remove from blender and place in a bowl.

4. Using a spoon, mix in capers and transfer to serving dish.

5. Cover tightly with plastic wrap and refrigerate for 2 hours minimum.

6. Serve with assorted crackers.

Steamed Clams or Mussels

Serves 8 as an appetizer, or 4 as the main course. Prep time: 30 minutes, plus 2 hours for cleaning clams if needed.

This recipe uses live Pacific Coast hard-shell littleneck clams (native littleneck, native butter, or manila). Mussels can also be used. If you harvest your own, be sure to follow state harvesting laws regarding procedures and licensing. Also check for up-to-date information regarding areas closed due to paralytic shellfish poisoning (PSP) or other contaminants. Purchased commercial shellfish will have been tested and inspected.

Clams and mussels that are purchased in the markets have generally been cleaned to remove the grit, but ask before purchasing. To remove grit from the clams, place clams in a bucket filled with cold water, ½ cup salt (not iodized), and ½ cup cornmeal per gallon of water. Water should cover clams. Let sit for 1 hour then drain water and replace with a new batch of water, salt, and cornmeal. Let sit 1 more hour, then drain and rinse well. If using mussels, they have a "beard" at the edge where the 2 shell halves come together. Cut off the beard with scissors. Both clams and mussels should be scrubbed under cold running water using a stiff brush. Discard any open, damaged, empty, or sand-filled shells. Once cleaned, clams and mussels can be refrigerated for 1 or 2 days if placed in a damp, towel-covered bowl.

4 pounds clams or mussels

2 tablespoons butter

2 cloves garlic, crushed

2 cups dry white wine

¼ cup heavy cream

1 teaspoon freshly ground white pepper

½ cup finely chopped fresh parsley for garnish

Melted butter, for dipping

Artisan bread, sliced, for dipping in broth

1. If necessary, let clams spit and self-clean for 2 hours before proceeding, per instructions above.

2. In a large stockpot over medium heat, add butter and garlic and cook until softened.

3. Add wine and bring to a boil.

4. Add clams or mussels and reduce heat to medium low. Cover and steam for about 5 minutes or until all clams or mussels have opened. Discard any that have not opened. (Some need longer to cook, so you might try steaming unopened ones about 2 minutes longer.)

5. Using a large slotted spoon, remove clams or mussels from the pot, leaving broth.

6. Let broth settle for a minute then slowly pour off most of the broth to another smaller pot, leaving any sand or bits of shell behind.

7. Heat the saved broth on low and add cream to broth; stir until broth is warm.

8. For individual servings, divide clams or mussels equally into bowls, and pour broth over. (To serve family style, just put them in a large bowl with a ladle, and pour in broth.)

9. Top with chopped parsley.

10. Serve with melted butter and bread.

11. Provide a dish or dishes to hold discarded shells.

Stuffed Phyllo Rolls

Makes 75 appetizers. Prep time: about 1 hour and 15 minutes, plus 30 minutes to bake.

This popular recipe uses phyllo dough, which can be found in the freezer section of most large grocery stores. It comes in 1-pound packages in various sheet sizes (from 5-inch squares to 14 x 16 inches). For this recipe you can use one of the small squares per appetizer or, if you use the larger size, cut into 4-inch or 5-inch squares. Follow the directions on the package, as phyllo dough is difficult if not impossible to work with when frozen or too dry. Always use one sheet at a time and keep the rest covered with wax paper and a damp tea towel to keep the thin sheets from drying out. You may have more dough sheets than you need for this recipe; if so, freeze leftover sheets for later use or discard. The rolls can be premade and frozen for baking later. To freeze, place them on a sheet pan without touching each other and freeze. When frozen, transfer them to quart- or gallon-sized freezer bags and return to freezer.

Filling:

¼ cup olive oil

2 tablespoons butter

1 bunch green onions, chopped

2 cloves garlic, crushed

2 pounds lean ground beef

1 teaspoon sea salt

1 teaspoon ground black pepper

¼ teaspoon ground allspice

1 teaspoon ground cinnamon

1 cup red wine

¼ cup tomato paste

½ cup water

½ cup finely chopped parsley

2 large eggs, slightly beaten

Phyllo:

1 pound salted butter

1 pound phyllo sheets, thawed

Prepare filling:

1. In a large skillet over medium heat, melt 2 tablespoons of butter with oil.

2. Add onions and garlic and cook, stirring, until translucent.

3. Add ground beef and spices and cook until brown, stirring to break up meat.

4. Pour off fat.

5. Add wine, tomato paste, water, and parsley; stir to combine.

6. Simmer for about 20 minutes or until most of the liquid has evaporated.

7. Remove from heat and allow mixture to cool thoroughly.

8. When cool, add eggs and mix well. Set aside.

Assemble and bake appetizers:

1. Melt 1 pound butter and keep warm.

2. Unroll thawed phyllo and lay out on cutting board. Cut sheets into 4-inch or 5-inch squares. Keep covered with the damp tea towel.

3. Prepare one appetizer at a time: Lay out one piece of phyllo dough and brush with melted butter. Re-cover remaining phyllo dough with tea towel.

4. Spoon 1 heaping teaspoon of meat filling into center of dough piece.

5. Fold near edge of dough over top of the filling then fold in the ends.

6. Roll tightly and place on a buttered, rimmed baking sheet.

7. Repeat until all filling is used. Transfer phyllo rolls to refrigerator.

8. Preheat oven to 325 degrees F.

9. Remove phyllo rolls from refrigerator, brush tops with melted butter, and place in oven.

10. Bake for 30 minutes or until brown. Serve warm.

Dill Weed Dip

Serves 6. Prep time: 10 minutes, plus chilling time (2 hours to overnight).

This dip can be made a day ahead of time and refrigerated. Use fresh raw vegetables for dipping.

1 cup sour cream

¼ cup finely chopped green onion

¼ cup finely chopped fresh dill weed

1 tablespoon fish sauce

¼ teaspoon freshly ground black pepper

1. Place all ingredients into a medium bowl and mix.

2. Refrigerate for 2 hours minimum.

Shrimp Dip

Serves 6. Prep time: 10 minutes, plus chilling time (2 hours to overnight).

Make this dip a day ahead of time to better blend the flavors. Serve with crackers or in sandwiches.

1 cup cooked finely chopped shrimp meat

1 (8 ounce) package cream cheese, softened

¼ cup finely chopped green onion

1 tablespoon finely chopped fresh parsley

1 tablespoon fish sauce

½ teaspoon freshly ground black pepper

1. Place all ingredients into a blender or food processor fitted with the steel blade.

2. Process until mixture is smooth.

3. Remove from blender and place in a bowl.

4. Cover tightly and refrigerate for 2 hours minimum.

5. Serve with assorted crackers.

Guacamole

Serves 2. Prep time: 8 minutes.

Avocado browns quickly when exposed to air. If you can't serve immediately, pack prepared guacamole in a bowl, level the top, pour a thin layer of olive oil over the top, and refrigerate. Before serving, pour off oil. Enjoy guacamole with corn chips, in sandwiches, or as a side in Mexican dishes.

1 large ripe avocado

½ cup finely chopped yellow onion

1 tablespoon fresh lemon juice

¼ teaspoon sea salt

¼ teaspoon freshly ground black pepper

Dash of hot sauce (I prefer Tabasco)

1. Peel and slice avocado.
2. Place avocado pieces in a small bowl and mash with fork.
3. Add remaining ingredients and mix well.
4. Serve immediately.

Layered Taco Dip

Serves 8. Prep time: 30 minutes, plus 30 minutes for chilling.

This is a great dish to take to a party. Be sure and take the tortilla chips too.

Avocado layer:

2 ripe avocados, halved and peeled, seeds removed

1 tablespoon fresh lemon juice

¼ cup onion juice (place one peeled large yellow onion in a blender and puree; then using a sieve, pour off onion juice and discard pulp)

¼ teaspoon iodized salt

½ teaspoon ground black pepper

Sour cream layer:

½ cup sour cream

¼ cup mayonnaise

1 teaspoon chili powder

½ teaspoon cornstarch

½ teaspoon ground red pepper

½ teaspoon garlic juice (place one peeled garlic clove in a garlic press and press out juice)

¼ teaspoon chopped fresh oregano

½ teaspoon ground cumin

Remaining layers:

2 cups Refried Beans (page 91) or one small can of refried beans plus ½ cup drained diced tomatoes with chilies

1 cup minced green onions (about 1 bunch)

1 large tomato, cored and chopped

1 (6 ounce) can pitted half or whole black olives, drained and chopped

½ cup shredded sharp cheddar cheese

2 slices bacon, cooked crisp and crumbled

Avocado layer:

1. In a small bowl, mash avocado with other ingredients and set aside.

Sour cream layer:

1. In a small bowl mix all ingredients for sour cream layer and set aside.

Assemble the layers:

1. In an 8 x 8-inch glass dish, evenly spread refried beans.

2. Add avocado mix, spreading evenly, then spread sour cream mix in a layer on top of that.

3. In layers, sprinkle green onions then tomatoes, olives, cheese, and bacon.

4. Cover and refrigerate for a minimum of 30 minutes.

5. Serve with tortilla chips.

Onion Dip

Serves 8. Prep time: 5 minutes.

Serve this dip with potato chips. Since it is quick and easy to make, you can fix this to serve for those panic situations!

1 (1 ounce) package dried onion soup mix

2 cups (16 ounces) sour cream

Dash of hot sauce (I prefer Tabasco)

1. Mix ingredients together in a small bowl.

2. Cover and refrigerate until ready to serve.

Roasted Garlic

Serves about 8. Prep time: 45 minutes.

Roasting garlic removes its strong, bitter taste. Serve soft cloves with toasted or grilled artisan bread and enjoy.

8 large garlic bulbs (6 to 10 cloves each, depending on the type of garlic)

¼ cup olive oil

1 tablespoon minced fresh thyme

1. Preheat oven to 350 degrees F.
2. Remove loose skins from garlic. Do not peel.
3. Cut off top of garlic bulb (the pointed end) to expose clove tops.
4. Remove fine roots on bottom of bulb and trim if necessary so bulb will sit without falling over.
5. Place bulbs on a cookie sheet with root end down.
6. Drizzle each bulb with oil and sprinkle with thyme.
7. Cover tightly with aluminum foil.
8. Place in preheated oven and cook for 20 minutes.
9. Uncover and bake an additional 15 minutes or until cloves are very soft and medium golden in color.

Salads and Soups

This section contains recipes for salads, salad dressings, and soups. I have not included simple green salads that you can make from various lettuces and other salad ingredients; rather, you'll find several classic American salads as well as salads that can be served as a main course. If you do grow some of your own salad ingredients, then use what you have in the garden in whatever combination you desire. Especially delicious in spring is freshly cut leaf lettuce served with cream, salt, and pepper—sometimes simple is best.

I have included only one oil and vinegar recipe in this section, as there are endless combinations. You may enjoy developing your own recipes: start with three parts oil to one part vinegar, using any type of vegetable oil and any type of vinegar that you want, plus salt and ground black or white pepper to taste. You can add many other ingredients, such as garlic, onion, or peppers. Whisk together in a glass or stainless steel bowl or use a blender if you want to puree the chunky ingredients.

Nothing is better than a pot of hot soup on the stove in fall and winter. Soups are a good way to use vegetables or meat nearing their end in the garden or refrigerator. You should always have chicken, beef, and vegetable stock on hand, as well as frozen or canned tomatoes to easily turn extra ingredients into soup. Cream soups are generally made by cooking the vegetable(s) in a small amount of water then cooling and pureeing them in a blender or food processor. The puree is then reheated with milk or cream.

I have never served cold soups even though I have enjoyed them when I have eaten them elsewhere. The cream soups I have included can all be eaten cold if you prefer.

If a soup recipe makes more that you can use at one time, freeze the rest in pint- or quart-sized freezer bags to heat and enjoy later when you need a quick and satisfying meal.

Coleslaw

Serves 6. Prep time: about 15 minutes.

The dressing part of this recipe can be made ahead of time and refrigerated for later use within one month. Coleslaw is popular served as a side to dishes like Fish and Chips (page 100) or in sandwiches in lieu of lettuce.

Dressing:

½ cup mayonnaise

1 tablespoon apple cider vinegar

½ teaspoon sugar

½ teaspoon celery salt

¼ teaspoon iodized salt

¼ teaspoon ground black pepper

Slaw:

½ medium-sized head green cabbage

½ green bell pepper

½ red bell pepper

1 small carrot

1 small yellow onion

1. Mix dressing ingredients together and set aside.

2. Remove outer leaves from cabbage and cut out core. Thinly slice cabbage and place in a large bowl.

3. Remove seeds and membranes from peppers and slice finely. Add to bowl.

4. Peel carrot and shred with a cheese grater into bowl.

5. Peel and chop onion finely. Add to bowl.

6. Add dressing to vegetables, and mix all ingredients well.

7. Cover tightly and refrigerate until ready to serve.

Greek Salad

Serves 6. Prep time: 15 minutes.

This is a delicious Mediterranean salad. Serve as either the salad course to a meal or as the main dish.

Salad:

1 head romaine lettuce

2 Roma tomatoes

1 cucumber

4 green onions

¼ cup chopped fresh parsley

½ cup feta cheese

12 pitted Greek olives

Dressing:

½ cup olive oil

¼ cup red wine vinegar

2 tablespoons fresh lemon juice

2 cloves garlic, crushed

2 teaspoons chopped fresh mint

1 teaspoon sea salt

1 teaspoon freshly ground white pepper

1. Remove outer romaine leaves and discard.

2. Wash romaine and dry thoroughly.

3. Tear romaine leaves and place in large salad bowl.

4. Wash tomatoes, core, slice into wedges, and place in salad bowl.

5. Wash cucumber and cut off ends.

6. Using a fork, deeply scratch cucumber peel from one end to the other; repeat until all of the peel has been scratched.

7. Slice cucumber and add to salad bowl.

8. Remove roots from green onions, wash, chop, and add to salad.

9. Wash and chop parsley and add to salad.

10. Place all of dressing ingredients in a blender and blend.

11. Pour dressing over salad and toss.

12. Top salad with feta cheese and Greek olives.

Molded Vegetable Salad

*Serves 8. Prep time: About 1 hour and 45 minutes from step 1 to step 6,
then a minimum of 4 hours (or overnight) in the refrigerator.*

This is a very light and refreshing salad; it can be made a day or two ahead. Molding dishes can be a 7 x 11-inch glass baking dish, a large decorative gelatin mold, or individual 6 ounce glass custard cups. I often serve this as the salad for Christmas dinner, but it is popular any time of the year.

2 (3 ounce) packages lemon gelatin, regular or sugar-free (I use sugar-free Jell-O)

2 cups boiling water

1½ cups cold water

¼ cup distilled white vinegar

1 teaspoon iodized salt

1 teaspoon freshly ground white pepper

2 tablespoons finely chopped green scallions (about 3)

½ cup finely chopped green pepper (about half a large pepper)

1 cup finely chopped celery (about 2 stalks)

½ cup finely chopped radishes (about 4)

¼ cup finely grated carrot (1 small carrot)

2 cups finely chopped cabbage (about ¼ head)

1 teaspoon horseradish

Dollop of mayonnaise for each serving

Dash of paprika, for garnish

Lettuce leaves, for bedding individual servings

1. Place gelatin in large mixing bowl and add boiling water, stirring until dissolved.

2. Add cold water, vinegar, salt, and pepper.

3. Stir and place in refrigerator until gelatin begins to set.

4. In a large bowl, mix all of the finely chopped vegetables with horseradish; cover and set aside in the refrigerator.

5. When gelatin has started to set, add vegetable mixture. Mix well to distribute throughout gelatin.

6. Place mixture in molding dish or dishes (see below for options), cover with plastic, and refrigerate until gelatin has completely set (about 4 hours).

Serving Suggestions:

1. For a 7 x 11-inch baking dish: Place a lettuce leaf on each individual serving dish. Cut molded salad into individual portions and use a metal spatula to transfer pieces onto leaves. Top with dollop of mayonnaise and dash of paprika.

2. For a decorative gelatin mold: Cover a serving plate the size of the mold with lettuce leaves. Remove salad from molding dish by immersing the bottom of the dish in hot water (up to the top of the gelatin) for about 10 seconds. Invert molded salad onto lettuce-lined serving dish. Top with thin layer of mayonnaise and sprinkle with paprika. To serve, cut off slices.

3. For individual custard cups: Cover each serving plate with a lettuce leaf. To remove salad from custard cups, immerse bottom of the cup in hot water (up to the top of the gelatin) for about 10 seconds. Invert molded salads onto serving plates. Top each with dollop of mayonnaise and dash of paprika.

Pasta Salad

Serves 12. Prep time: about 1 hour.

This salad is better if premade a day before serving to allow the pasta to absorb the liquids and improve the flavor. My family loves this recipe!

1 (22 ounce) package of small seashell pasta

2 quarts water (for cooking pasta)

1 tablespoon olive oil (for cooking pasta)

1 teaspoon iodized salt (for cooking pasta)

2 hard-boiled eggs

1 cup finely chopped yellow onion

1 cup finely diced celery

1 cup finely chopped bread and butter pickles (try my Bread and Butter Pickles recipe on page 180)

¼ cup bread and butter pickle juice (stir pickle juice in jar to mix all ingredients before pouring off the juice)

1 can (5.75 ounces) pitted black olives

½ pound mild cheddar cheese, cut into ¼-inch cubes

1 cup mayonnaise

¼ cup prepared mustard

1 teaspoon celery salt

1 teaspoon iodized salt

1 teaspoon ground black pepper

8 leaves lettuce or kale, for trimming the serving dish

1 tablespoon paprika

1. Cook pasta shells in large pot with 2 quarts water, olive oil, and salt per directions on the bag until they're al dente. Drain and rinse with cold water until cooked pasta is cool. Allow to drain, shake off excess water, stir thoroughly, and refrigerate. This can be done ahead of time.

2. Simmer eggs in hot (not boiling) water for 10 minutes. Remove from hot water and rinse in cold water until thoroughly cool. Refrigerate. This can also be done ahead of time.

3. Transfer pasta shells to a large mixing bowl.

4. Peel and chop boiled eggs and add to bowl.

5. Add remaining ingredients (except paprika and lettuce) and mix until blended. Add more pickle juice and/or mayonnaise if mixture is too dry. Cover and refrigerate until ready to serve.

6. Before serving, stir salad and, again, add pickle juice or mayonnaise if too dry.

7. Transfer pasta salad to a serving dish lined with lettuce or kale.

8. Top with paprika; cover and refrigerate until ready to serve.

Potato Salad

Serves 8. Prep time: ½ hour, assuming potatoes and eggs are cooked beforehand.

Potato salad should be made the day before serving to allow the potatoes to absorb the liquids and improve the flavor. This is a popular dish to take to a potluck picnic, but keep it cold by packing the serving dish in ice and keeping it in the shade.

3 pounds Yukon Gold or other waxy potatoes (about 8 medium)

2 hard-boiled eggs

1 cup finely chopped yellow onion (one small onion)

1 cup finely chopped bread and butter pickles (try my Bread and Butter Pickles recipe on page 180)

¼ cup bread and butter pickle juice (stir pickle juice in jar to mix all ingredients before pouring off juice)

1 cup mayonnaise

¼ cup prepared mustard

1 teaspoon celery salt

1 teaspoon iodized salt

1 teaspoon ground black pepper

8 leaves lettuce or kale, for trimming serving dish

1 tablespoon paprika

1. Clean potatoes (do not peel) and place them in a large pot; cover with water and cook over low heat, but do not allow to boil. Pierce potatoes in the center with a fork; remove from heat when they are tender (do not overcook). Drain then refrigerate uncovered until totally cooled. (This is best if done a day ahead since the potatoes take a while to cool and lose moisture in the refrigerator.)

2. Simmer eggs in hot (not boiling) water for 10 minutes. Remove from hot water and rinse in cold water until thoroughly cool. Refrigerate. This can also be done ahead of time.

3. In a large bowl, peel and slice potatoes. Discard peels.

4. Peel and chop hard-boiled eggs and add to bowl.

5. Add remaining ingredients (except paprika and lettuce) and mix until blended.

6. Transfer to serving dish lined with lettuce or kale.

7. Top with paprika; cover and refrigerate until ready to serve.

Oil and Vinegar Salad Dressing

Serves 6. Prep time: 5 minutes.

Use this versatile dressing over green salads or drizzle over chicken pieces or fish fillets while grilling.

⅓ cup apple cider or balsamic vinegar

½ teaspoon sugar

1 tablespoon finely chopped fresh parsley

1 teaspoon iodized salt

1 teaspoon freshly ground white pepper

1 teaspoon crushed red pepper flakes

¾ cup pure olive oil

1. In small glass or stainless steel bowl, combine all ingredients except oil.

2. Using a fork or whisk, slowly add oil to the bowl and beat until well mixed.

3. Serve as desired; refrigerate remaining dressing for later use.

Poppy Seed Salad Dressing

Serves 6. Prep time: 5 minutes.

Use this dressing over green salad or fresh fruit. The poppy seeds in this dressing give it an interesting texture.

$^1/_3$ cup apple cider vinegar

2 teaspoons sugar

1½ tablespoons onion juice (place ½ peeled large yellow onion in a blender and puree; then, using a sieve, pour off onion juice and discard pulp)

1 teaspoon iodized salt

1 teaspoon dry mustard

1 cup extra virgin olive oil

2 tablespoons poppy seeds

1. In a blender, combine all ingredients except oil and poppy seeds.

2. Blend until well mixed then drizzle in oil while continuing to blend.

3. Remove from blender and stir in poppy seeds.

4. Refrigerate until ready to serve.

Ranch Dressing

Serves 12 (about 1 pint). Prep time: 15 minutes.

Use this dressing over green salad or as a dip. The red bell pepper makes dressing somewhat red. If you prefer a more cream- or green- colored dressing, use green pepper instead.

½ cup mayonnaise

¼ cup sour cream

½ cup buttermilk

1 teaspoon apple cider vinegar

¼ cup diced red bell pepper

2 green onions, minced

1 clove garlic, minced

1 tablespoon minced fresh parsley

1 teaspoon iodized salt

1 teaspoon freshly ground white pepper

1. Combine all ingredients in a blender and mix.
2. Cover tightly and refrigerate until ready to serve.

Thousand Island Dressing

Serves 4 (about 1 cup). Prep time: 15 minutes.

Use this dressing over green salad or use in a main course chef's salad, crab Louis, or shrimp Louis, or slather on hamburger buns in lieu of mayonnaise.

1 large egg

½ cup mayonnaise

3 tablespoons bottled chili sauce (or substitute ketchup in a pinch)

1 tablespoon 2 percent milk

2 tablespoons minced bread and butter pickles

1 tablespoon minced fresh parsley

1 teaspoon paprika

1 teaspoon hot sauce (I prefer Tabasco)

1 teaspoon freshly ground white pepper

1. Simmer egg in hot (not boiling) water for 10 minutes. Remove and rinse in cold water until thoroughly cool.

2. Peel and finely dice egg.

3. In a small mixing bowl combine diced egg with all other ingredients.

4. Cover and refrigerate until ready to serve.

Chicken Broth

Makes about 2 quarts. Prep time: 2 hours plus overnight in the refrigerator.

This broth is made from the chicken parts, including skin, left over after removing legs, thighs, wings, and breast from a whole chicken. Buying whole chickens is considerably less expensive than buying chicken parts, and you get the main ingredient for this great broth that can be used immediately or frozen for later use in soups or other dishes.

1 whole chicken

2 quarts water (use bottled water if your tap water tastes bad)

Iodized salt and ground black pepper

1. Wash chicken under cold running water. Remove legs, thighs, breast halves, and wings. Remove skin from thighs and breast pieces. (Legs, thighs, breast, and wings are not used in this broth recipe. They can be frozen for use later or used fresh for fried or grilled chicken. *Note: After handling raw chicken, clean your hands and all surfaces and utensils with disinfecting soap to prevent salmonella contamination.)*

2. Place remaining chicken carcass, including skin, in a large pot and cover with 2 quarts water. Bring to a boil. Reduce heat to low and simmer for approximately 1½ hours.

3. Remove from heat and strain broth through a colander into another pot.

4. Let chicken parts, bones, and skin cool until pieces can be handled without burning your fingers. Carefully remove bits and pieces of chicken meat from the bones and dice into pieces; add them to broth. Discard remaining carcass bones and skin.

5. Refrigerate broth overnight.

6. Remove broth from refrigerator. The fat will have congealed on top of the broth. Carefully remove congealed fat with a spoon and discard it.

7. The broth can now be heated for use in other recipes (add iodized salt and ground white pepper to taste) or frozen for later use. Most of my uses for broth include broth with chicken bits and pieces of meat. If you want broth without chicken bits and pieces of meat, run broth through a sieve to separate.

Chicken Dumplings

Serves 4. Prep time: 20 minutes.

This was my Grandmother Elsie Wilson's recipe. She called it "Pootski" (a nod to her Czecho-slovakian heritage). This is a good hardy dish for those cool spring days. It uses the early spring volunteer dill weed that comes up in the garden. If you have leftover fried or grilled chicken, you can remove the cooked meat from the skin and bones, dice, and add to broth.

2 quarts chicken broth (recipe above) or (in a pinch) purchased chicken broth

4 large eggs, beaten

1½ cups all-purpose flour

½ cup chopped yellow onion

¼ cup chopped fresh dill weed or 2 tablespoons dried if you don't have fresh

Iodized salt and ground black pepper

1. In a large pot, heat chicken broth to boiling. Reduce heat to medium.

2. In a separate bowl, mix eggs, flour, onion, and dill weed to make dumpling dough.

3. Drop dough in tablespoon-sized pieces one at a time into boiling broth.

4. Dough will rise to the top of the broth when cooked (about 3 minutes after the last piece is dropped).

5. Reduce heat to simmer. Add salt and pepper to taste and serve.

Chicken Noodle Soup

Serves 6. Prep time: 45 minutes.

This is a hardy soup for cold days, and a good way to use up the last of the pepper/chili crop from the garden.

2 cups diced chicken meat (either previously cooked or raw)

1 large leek, sliced into chunks

1 carrot, cut into ¼-inch slices

½ red bell pepper, cut into small chunks

½ sweet red pepper, such as Corno di Toro or Pimento cut into small chunks

1 tablespoon chopped fresh thyme

2 (14.5 ounce) cans chicken broth

2 cups water

2 cups dried egg noodles

1 teaspoon freshly ground white pepper

1 teaspoon turmeric

1 tablespoon paprika

Iodized salt to taste

1. Place all ingredients in a large pot and bring to a boil.
2. Reduce heat to medium low and simmer for ½ hour.

Caldillo: Mexican Stew

Serves 6. Prep time: about 3 hours.

This recipe is adapted from a recipe from my friend and neighbor Martha Overall. It is a hit for tailgate parties or Super Bowl Sunday.

3 pounds round or chuck steak

2 strips bacon, cut into small pieces

1 large yellow onion, diced

2 cloves garlic, crushed

1 large green chili, such as Anaheim, diced

3 cups cored, peeled, and diced tomatoes or 1 (28 ounce) can, undrained

1 (14.5 ounce) can beef broth

1 (14.5 ounce) can chicken broth

1 teaspoon iodized salt

2 teaspoons freshly ground black pepper

2 teaspoons ground cumin

1. Cut beef into ½- to ¾-inch cubes, removing and discarding fat and gristle.

2. Cook the bacon for 2 minutes in a large Dutch oven or stockpot over medium heat.

3. Leaving bacon pieces in, add beef and brown.

4. Add onion, garlic, and chili and cook until tender.

5. Add remaining ingredients and bring to a boil.

6. Reduce heat to low and simmer for 2½ hours or until meat is tender. *Note: Simmering will allow the stew to thicken. When the stew has thickened to sauce consistency, cover pot with a lid to prevent further thickening.*

Chili with Beans

Serves 6. Preptime: about 1 hour, plus about 3 hours for cooking.

This chili is great to serve on a cold day. I like to top off each bowl with a large spoonful of cottage cheese. You can also top with grated cheese, sour cream, or ricotta cheese. Garnish with chopped green onions or chives if you like. Take this to football tailgate parties.

2 cups dry pinto beans

1 slice raw bacon, cut into small pieces

1 pound hamburger meat (20 percent fat)

1 large yellow onion, chopped

2 cloves garlic, crushed

2 cups homemade Salsa (page 175) or use 1 (10 ounce) can diced tomatoes and green chilies

1 (14.5 ounce) can chicken broth

1 (14.5 ounce) can beef broth

1 (8 ounce) can tomato sauce

2 cups water

1 teaspoon iodized salt

1 teaspoon freshly ground black pepper

1 teaspoon oregano

1 tablespoon cumin

1 tablespoon chili powder

1 bay leaf, fresh or dried

1 jalapeño pepper, chopped

2 small peppers (one red, such as pimento and one green, such as Anaheim), seeds removed and cut into small pieces

4 fresh or dried serrano chilies, cut into small pieces, with seeds

1. Wash and remove dirt, sticks, and cracked/broken beans from beans.

2. Place beans with 1 quart (4 cups) water in a large stockpot or Dutch oven. Bring to just boiling then drain water from beans, discarding the water. Set beans aside.

3. Brown bacon in stockpot.

4. Leaving bacon in stockpot, add hamburger and cook until brown, breaking up into small pieces.

5. Drain off fat then add onions and garlic and cook for 1 minute, stirring.

6. Add beans, salsa, and remaining ingredients.

7. Stir and return mixture to boiling.

8. Place lid on pot, reduce heat to low and cook covered for 3 hours, stirring occasionally.

9. Ladle into bowls and garnish as desired.

Vegetable Beef Soup

Serves 8. Prep time: about 2 hours.

This is a great recipe for fall and winter, as it uses vegetables from the garden as well as a variety of frozen vegetables. If you're not hungry, smelling the aroma from this soup will quickly change your mind.

1 pound beef chuck or round steak cut into ½-inch cubes, fat and sinew removed

1 large onion, finely chopped

4 cloves garlic, crushed

1 bay leaf, fresh or dried

1 tablespoon fresh chopped thyme

1 tablespoon fresh chopped rosemary

1 tablespoon fresh minced parsley

1 teaspoon iodized salt

1 teaspoon ground black pepper

1 tablespoon Worcestershire sauce

2 (14.5 ounce) cans beef broth

1 stalk celery, cut into ¼-inch slices

1 cup frozen green beans

1 cup frozen corn

1 cup frozen peas

2 cups frozen tomatoes or 1 can (14 ounces) canned tomatoes

2 cups homemade Salsa (page 175) or use 1 (10 ounce) can diced tomatoes and green chilies

2 russet potatoes, peeled and diced into ¾-inch pieces

4 carrots, scraped or peeled and cut into ¼-inch slices

4 turnips, peeled and diced into ½-inch pieces

¾ cup raw elbow macaroni

1. Brown meat over medium heat in a large pot or Dutch oven.

2. Add onions and garlic and cook for 5 minutes, stirring.

3. Add remaining ingredients except for potatoes, carrots, turnips, and macaroni.

4. Bring to a boil while occasionally stirring until all frozen ingredients are thawed.

5. Reduce heat to low and simmer for 1 hour, stirring occasionally.

6. About 30 minutes before serving, add potatoes, carrots, turnips, and macaroni.

7. Increase heat until boiling resumes then lower heat to a simmer.

8. Serve when all vegetables and the macaroni are tender.

Cioppino: Seafood Stew

Serves 8. Prep time: about 1 hour and 45 minutes.

Cioppino is pronounced "chuh-PEE-no." It is a fisherman's seafood stew, so feel free to impro-vise, using the seafood that you have on hand or that is seasonal and fresh in the markets. Market-bought clams and mussels have usually been cleaned to remove the grit, but ask before purchasing. If you've harvested your own shellfish, see cleaning and safety instruc-tions for Steamed Clams or Mussels (page 12).

You can make the sauce and prep the seafood a day ahead; this will save about 1½ hours' time on the day you're serving the cioppino. This dish is one of my favorite dishes and it can also be used as the main course.

½ cup salted butter

1 large yellow onion, chopped

4 cloves garlic, minced

½ cup fresh parsley leaves, minced

1 quart fresh tomatoes, cored, peeled, and cut into pieces (or use 1 quart of frozen toma-toes, or 2 [14.5 ounce] cans tomatoes)

2 (8 ounce) bottles clam juice

1 (14.5 ounce) can chicken broth

2 bay leaves, fresh or dried

1 tablespoon chopped fresh basil leaves

1 teaspoon minced fresh rosemary

1 teaspoon minced fresh thyme

1 teaspoon minced fresh oregano leaves

2 cups dry red wine

1 pound small hard-shell clams, cleaned

1 pound mussels, cleaned and debearded

1½ pounds cooked tail-on medium shrimp

1½ pounds halibut, cod, bass, flounder, haddock, or perch, bones removed and cut into 1-inch chunks

1½ cups cooked fresh flaked crabmeat

1 teaspoon sea salt

1 teaspoon ground black pepper

1. Melt butter in a large stockpot or cast-iron Dutch oven on medium-low heat; add onions, garlic, and parsley.

2. Cook slowly, stirring occasionally, until onions are softened.

3. Add tomatoes, clam juice, chicken broth, herbs, and wine.

4. Bring to a boil, reduce heat to low; cover, and simmer approximately 45 minutes to 1 hour. If sauce becomes too thick, thin with more tomato juice, clam juice, or chicken broth.

5. Proceed to next step or, if making sauce ahead of time, refrigerate until ready to use then reheat.

6. Clean clams and mussels if necessary. (See above.)

7. Add shrimp, fish, and crabmeat to the simmering sauce. Cover and simmer about 5 minutes, until clams and mussels open. Discard any that have not opened. (Sometimes they need to cook longer than 5 minutes to open, so you might try removing the unopened ones from the pot and steaming them in 1 cup of water for 2 minutes longer to be sure all of the live ones have opened. Do not overcook.)

8. Remove bay leaves; season with salt and pepper and adjust to taste.

9. Remove from heat and ladle broth and seafood into large soup bowls.

10. Provide bowls for disposal of shells.

11. Serve with sourdough bread for dipping into broth.

New England Clam Chowder

Serves 6 to 8. Prep time: about 45 minutes.

Any type of clam can be used for this chowder, including canned whole baby clams (which this recipe uses), canned clam pieces, or fresh clams. If you're using a larger species of fresh clam, it's best to grind the meat (to yield about 2 cups), since it tends to be tough. This soup can also serve as the main course. It seems to taste better on cold rainy days.

3 slices bacon, cut into small pieces

1 cup yellow onion, finely diced

1 cup finely diced celery

2 (10 ounce) cans baby clams

2 (8 ounce) bottles clam juice

3 medium russet potatoes, peeled and diced into ¼-inch cubes

1 teaspoon iodized salt

1 teaspoon freshly ground white pepper

2 tablespoons finely chopped fresh thyme

1 bay leaf, fresh or dried

1 tablespoon finely chopped fresh parsley

½ cup all-purpose flour

1 cup cold water

2 cups heavy cream

Parsley and/or chives, chopped for garnish

1. In a large pot over medium heat, cook bacon until crisp and remove.
2. Add onion and celery to bacon fat in the pot and cook until tender, without browning.
3. Add clams, clam juice, potatoes, and bacon.
4. Add salt, pepper, and herbs and bring to a boil.

5. Reduce heat to simmer and cook for 10 minutes or until potatoes are cooked, stirring occasionally.

6. In a small bowl, whisk flour with cold water until lumps are gone.

7. Add flour mixture to the pot and stir to mix, simmering until chowder thickens.

8. Add cream and stir until chowder is well heated.

9. Remove bay leaf.

10. Ladle chowder into serving bowls and top with parsley and/or chives.

Cream of Broccoli Soup

Serves 6. Prep time: about 30 minutes.

This light and creamy soup is very easy and quick to make.

4 cups chopped broccoli (or substitute cauliflower if desired)

2 cups chopped yellow onion (about 1 large)

2 chopped cloves garlic

2 (14.5 ounce) cans chicken broth

1 teaspoon minced fresh thyme

1 bay leaf fresh or dried

¼ cup butter

¼ cup all-purpose flour

½ teaspoon iodized salt

½ teaspoon ground white pepper

2 cups 2 percent milk

2 cups shredded sharp cheddar cheese

1. In a large pot, combine first 6 ingredients and bring to a boil. Reduce heat and simmer for 10 minutes.

2. Remove bay leaf.

3. Carefully pour mixture into a food processor or blender and pulse until smooth. Set aside.

4. In original pot over medium heat, melt butter and whisk in flour, salt, and pepper until mixture is bubbly.

5. Gradually add milk, stirring until mixture thickens.

6. Add cheese, stirring until melted and mixed.

7. Add broccoli mixture from food processor or blender.

8. Stir and heat briefly. Adjust salt and pepper to taste.

Lentil Soup

Serves 6. Prep time: about 1 hour.

Lentils are loaded with protein, fiber, iron, zinc, potassium, and magnesium. They are called pulses, which are legumes, as are dry peas and chickpeas (garbanzo beans). Try this recipe if you've never had lentils; you will enjoy.

1 pound brown lentils (2 cups), washed and drained

1 cup diced ham

5 cups water

1 (14.5 ounce) can beef broth

1 cup diced yellow onion

2 cloves garlic, minced

1 teaspoon iodized salt

1 teaspoon freshly ground black pepper

1. Place all ingredients in a large Dutch oven or stockpot and bring to a boil.

2. Reduce heat to low; cover and simmer for 45 minutes, stirring occasionally.

Bean Soup

Serves 4. Prep time: 2 ½ hours.

I generally use pinto or great northern beans for this hearty soup, but any dried beans can be used. Bean soup freezes well, so you might plan on doubling this recipe and freezing half for a satisfying, quick nutritious meal when you need something fast.

2 cups dried beans

2 quarts water, divided

2 slices raw bacon, cut into small pieces (or substitute one ham bone)

½ large yellow onion, chopped

2 cloves garlic, crushed

1 (14.5 ounce) can chicken broth

1 (14.5 ounce) can beef broth

1 teaspoon freshly ground black pepper

Iodized salt to taste

1. Wash beans and remove dirt, sticks, and cracked/broken beans.

2. Place beans with 1 quart of the water in a large stock-pot or Dutch oven. Bring to just boiling then drain water from beans, discarding the water.

3. Return beans to the pot over medium heat and add the second quart of water.

4. Add remaining ingredients and cover.

5. Bring mixture to a boil then reduce heat to medium low and cook for about 2 hours, until beans are soft, adding salt to taste.

6. Before serving, remove ham bone (if using), pick any meat away, and add to soup. Discard bone.

Potato Soup

Serves 6 to 8. Prep time: about 35 minutes.

Make potato soup when you think you have nothing else to serve. Chances are you will have all these ingredients on hand.

3 slices bacon, cut into small pieces

1 cup finely diced yellow onion

1 cup finely diced celery

1 (14.5 ounce) can chicken broth

4 medium russet potatoes, peeled and sliced ¼-inch thick

1 teaspoon iodized salt

1 teaspoon freshly ground white pepper

2 tablespoons finely chopped fresh thyme

1 tablespoon finely chopped fresh parsley

3 cups 2 percent milk

2 tablespoons butter

½ cup all-purpose flour

1 cup cold water

Chopped parsley and/or chives, for garnish

1. In a large pot over medium heat, cook bacon until crisp and remove.
2. Add onion and celery to bacon fat in pot and cook until tender, without browning.
3. Add chicken broth, potatoes, and bacon.
4. Add salt, pepper, and herbs and bring to a boil.
5. Continue cooking over medium heat for 10 minutes or until potatoes are cooked, stirring occasionally.
6. Add milk and butter, stirring until soup is heated to near boiling.
7. In a small bowl, whisk the flour with cold water until all of the lumps are gone.
8. Add flour mixture to soup and stir to mix, simmering until soup thickens.
9. Allow to cook for 5 minutes, but do not let soup boil.
10. Ladle soup into serving bowls and top with parsley and/or chives.

Split Pea Soup

Serves 4. Prep time: about 1 hour.

Split pea soup is very nutritious and hardy and can be served as the main course.

1 pound (2 cups) dried green split peas, washed and drained

1 cup diced cooked ham or small ham bone

2 cups water

1 (14.5 ounce) can chicken broth

½ cup diced celery

½ cup diced yellow onion

½ cup diced carrot

1 clove garlic, minced

1 teaspoon iodized salt

1 teaspoon freshly ground white pepper

1 cup half-and-half

1. Place all ingredients except half-and-half in a large pot and bring to a boil.

2. Reduce heat to medium low and simmer for 45 minutes, stirring occasionally. If you used a ham bone, remove bone and discard at the end of this step.

3. Add half-and-half and stir. If soup is too thick, add water.

4. Continue heating for 5 minutes before serving; do not let the soup come to a boil.

Main Dishes

The following recipes were mainstays for the dinners I prepared over thirty-five years. Some are main courses and others side dishes; some were used for everyday meals and others for special occasions. I have omitted many items that I served as main dishes because I assume you know how to make hamburgers, grilled or baked meats, and basic fish and vegetable dishes. All of these recipes use common ingredients that are, for the most part, very economical. Most can be made quickly and require no special kitchen tools.

I encourage you to try preparing the main dishes in various ways. If you have a slow cooker try making stews from meat you have on hand and adding vegetables from the garden. Also, it pays to get good at outdoor meat and vegetable grilling—grilled food is always popular and grilling imparts flavors that stove-top cooking or baking cannot.

I know it is difficult to come home after a long day at work and prepare a homemade meal with hungry kids asking every minute when dinner will be ready. I also know that it is easier to pick something up on the way home or cook something out of a box or can, but these meals are expensive and generally lack nutritional value. I opted to take the time to home cook dinners to provide good nutrition at reasonable cost, and you can too. Remember to take the meat out of the freezer and put in the refrigerator the night before!

Baked Stuffed Chicken Breasts

Serves 8. Prep time: about 20 minutes, plus 45 minutes for baking.

You can make this recipe a complete meal by adding ¾ cup of uncooked rice, peeled and cut potatoes, peeled and cut parsnips, and peeled carrots along the sides of the stuffed breasts in the baking dish.

8 chicken breast halves, skin and bones removed

8 slices provolone cheese

8 thin slices ham

1 (10¾ ounce) cream of chicken condensed soup

1 cup water

1 large egg, beaten

½ cup crushed soda crackers or Italian bread crumbs, or some of each

1 teaspoon paprika

1 teaspoon ground black pepper

1. Preheat oven to 375 degrees F.

2. Place one of the breast halves on a piece of plastic wrap.

3. Lay plastic over the breast meat and flatten using a mallet, or whack with the bottom of a small cast-iron skillet until the piece is about ½-inch thick.

4. Peel back plastic and add 1 piece of cheese and 1 piece of ham.

5. Roll up the chicken in ham and cheese slices and secure with a wooden toothpick. Repeat with remaining chicken pieces.

6. Dip each roll in beaten egg and then roll in crushed crackers or breadcrumbs.

7. Place in a 9 x 13-inch ovenproof baking dish.

8. In a medium bowl, mix the soup with water until well combined; pour it carefully along the sides of the breasts in the baking pan to avoid coating the tops of the breasts.

9. Sprinkle paprika and pepper on top of the rolled-up breasts and place in the oven.

10. Bake for 45 minutes or until breasts are brown and cooked through.

Chicken Chow Mein

Serves 12. Prep time: about 20 minutes,
assuming steps 1 through 4 are done ahead of time.

This makes a colorful, heaping platter of healthy, delicious food! You will need a wok for this recipe. If you don't have a wok, use a 12-inch or larger sauté pan with lid or aluminum foil cover and do the stir-frying in 2 batches.

1 (6 ounce) package fresh chow mein noodles (I prefer Sunluck)

1 whole chicken breast (2 large pieces)

Marinade:

1 tablespoon oyster sauce

1 teaspoon soy sauce

¼ teaspoon iodized salt

½ teaspoon ground black pepper

1 teaspoon cornstarch

Vegetables:

1 pound bean sprouts, rinsed and drained

2 celery stalks, chopped

1 small head green cabbage, cored and coarsely chopped in chunks

½ pound mushrooms, sliced

1 red bell pepper, seeds and veins removed, cut into chunks

½ yellow onion, cut into chunks

1 (8 ounce) can water chestnuts, rinsed and sliced

2 green onions or 1 small leek, chopped

Sauce:

½ cup chicken broth

1 tablespoon oyster sauce

1 tablespoon soy sauce

1 clove garlic, crushed

¼ teaspoon iodized salt

½ teaspoon ground black pepper

1 tablespoon cornstarch

Finishing:

4 tablespoons peanut oil, for stir-frying

2 tablespoons sesame seeds, for garnish

1. Boil noodles in water for 3 to 5 minutes or per instructions on package. Drain and rinse in cold water; refrigerate.

2. In a medium bowl, combine marinade ingredients. Remove skin and bones (save bones for step 3) from chicken breast. Cut chicken into small pieces and place in bowl with marinade. Mix and refrigerate.

3. Boil breastbones in 2 cups of water until water is reduced to ½ cup. Remove and discard bones. Refrigerate chicken broth for use in step 5.

4. Prepare all vegetables and refrigerate.

5. Prepare sauce by mixing all sauce ingredients in a small pan over medium heat. Once sauce has thickened, remove from heat but keep warm.

6. Heat wok over medium-high heat, and add 2 tablespoons peanut oil for stir-frying.

7. Drain excess marinade and add marinated chicken and stir-fry until brown. Remove cooked chicken onto paper towels and set aside in a warm place.

8. Add 2 more tablespoons oil to wok and add noodles, stir-frying until noodles are well heated.

9. Add all vegetables, chicken, and sauce. Cover wok with its lid and steam the contents for 5 minutes, stirring every minute and recovering, until cabbage is wilted and all ingredients are lightly cooked. (After the first minute, make sure there is enough moisture in the wok for steaming; if not, add ¼ cup water.)

10. Place chow mein on large serving platter and top with sesame seeds.

11. Serve immediately.

Honey Mustard Grilled Chicken

Serves 4. Prep time: about 10 minutes, plus 20 minutes for grilling.

The chicken is cooked on an outdoor grill. You can prepare the chicken and glaze the day before. Place the chicken and glaze in a sealable plastic bag and refrigerate until ready to grill. I like to start this recipe by cutting a whole chicken into parts; you can also use chicken parts that are already cut up, but they are generally quite a bit more expensive. If you can find thighs or hindquarters on sale, they can be used, as they provide uniform individual servings. If you want chicken gravy to serve with mashed potatoes on the side, use the skin removed from the chicken pieces in step 3 below. Fry chicken skins in a skillet until crisp then discard skins and fat, leaving 1 tablespoon of fat in the skillet. Add ¼ cup flour, stir to mix flour with fat, then drizzle in 1 cup heated milk, plus salt and pepper to taste. Stir over medium heat until thickened.

1 whole chicken, cut into pieces, breast cut in half

¼ cup Dijon mustard or use my Mustard (page 174)

¼ cup honey

2 tablespoons chopped fresh dill

2 tablespoons orange marmalade

1 tablespoon freshly grated orange peel

1 teaspoon iodized salt

1 teaspoon ground black pepper

1. Preheat grill to 375 degrees F.

2. In a small bowl, mix all ingredients together except chicken pieces.

3. Remove skin from chicken pieces and coat all sides with honey mustard mixture.

4. Place on preheated grill and cook for 10 minutes.

5. Turn pieces over and continue grilling for an additional 10 minutes or until done.

6. If any honey mustard mixture is left, use it to baste chicken at the end of the grilling time.

Beef Kebabs with Peanut Sauce

Serves 8. Prep time: about 1 hour.

These are cooked on an outdoor grill. You will need 8 stainless steel, wood, or bamboo skewers (presoak wood or bamboo skewers in water for at least 30 minutes to avoid burning). Feel free to change the vegetables that you use.

Marinated beef:

2 pounds beef (top round or sirloin steak)

¼ cup soy sauce

1 clove garlic, crushed

Kebab vegetables:

1 green bell pepper, cut into 16 pieces

1 red bell pepper, cut into 16 pieces

16 small purple onions or 16 chunks of yellow onion or use multiplier onions (see description, page 214)

2 zucchinis (approximately 8 inches long), cut into 16 pieces

8 small kohlrabies

8 small red beets

8 small red potatoes

Peanut sauce:

1 (13.5 ounce) can unsweetened coconut milk

1 cup creamy peanut butter

2 tablespoons fish sauce

2 teaspoons sriracha (hot chili sauce)

Salt and pepper

Topping:

¼ cup chopped roasted peanuts

2 small limes, cut into 8 pieces

1. Cut steak into ¼-inch-thick strips about 2 to 3 inches long; place in a medium bowl.

2. Add soy sauce and garlic to steak, stir to mix well, and set aside.

3. Wash and prepare green and red peppers, onions, zucchini, and kohlrabi.

4. In separate small pans, boil beets and potatoes until they are slightly tender, but not completely done. Drain and set aside.

5. In a medium-sized pan over medium heat, whisk all peanut sauce ingredients together until smooth and heated. Reduce heat to low and keep warm.

6. Clean, oil, and heat grill to 375 degrees F.

7. Skewer meat onto skewers by folding strips in half. Alternate with vegetables, including beets and potatoes, until all vegetables and meat have been used.

8. Season skewers with salt and pepper.

9. Place on grill and turn occasionally until meat is browned and cooked to medium, and vegetables are tender, about 8 minutes.

10. To serve, remove meat and vegetables from each skewer onto each of the 8 serving plates and top each with peanut sauce, chopped roasted peanuts, and a lime wedge.

Beef Stroganoff

Serves 6. Prep time: 30 minutes.

Beef stroganoff is quick and easy to make even if you forgot to take the meat out of the freezer the night before. If meat is frozen, place it in the microwave on defrost for 5 minutes, remove, and meat will be partially frozen and just right to slice.

1½ pounds of round steak or London broil, sliced into ⅛-inch-thin slices with fat removed (easier to slice thin if partially frozen)

4 cups dried egg noodles

½ cup finely chopped yellow onion

½ cup finely chopped red bell pepper or mild sweet pepper, such as pimento

2 cloves garlic, minced

1 (0.87 ounce) package beef gravy dry mix

½ cup cold water

1 (8 ounce) can mushroom stems and pieces, drained

2 tablespoons ketchup

½ cup red wine

1 teaspoon iodized salt

1 teaspoon freshly ground white pepper

1 cup sour cream

6 chopped green onions, for garnish

Meat:

1. In a large cast-iron skillet over medium heat, cook meat until browned.

2. Add onion, red pepper, and garlic to meat; cook, stirring, for 5 minutes.

3. Combine beef gravy mix with cold water and add to the cooking meat; stir.

4. Add mushrooms, ketchup, wine, salt, and pepper; stir. Cover pan; reduce heat to low and continue cooking for about another 5 minutes.

5. Remove from heat but keep warm. Just before serving, add sour cream and stir until well mixed.

Cook noodles at same time as meat:

1. In a large pot bring 2 quarts water to boil with 1 teaspoon salt and 1 tablespoon olive oil.

2. Add noodles and cook for about 5 minutes or until noodles are tender. Drain.

To serve:

1. Place noodles on plates and top with meat mixture.

2. Sprinkle each portion with chopped green onion.

Corned Beef and Cabbage

Serves 10. Prep time: about 7 hours.

I have cooked St. Patrick's Day dinner for years, and this is the recipe I use. If you like, you can also make Irish Soda Bread (page 152) to go with this meal. You will need a large pot with a lid (11 inches in diameter and 10 inches tall) that will hold all of the ingredients. For fewer servings, reduce amounts below accordingly; likewise, increase them if you need to serve more people.

7 to 8 pounds flat-cut corned beef (generally 2 packages)

1 large head green cabbage (about 4 pounds), cored and cut into quarters

3 pounds medium red potatoes (10 to 12), scrubbed, skins left on

2½ pounds carrots (10 to 12), peeled and cut in half crosswise

Butter, to serve with the vegetables

1. Fill large pot about ¹/₃ full with water. Add the corned beef, along with the spice package generally included in each package.

2. Cover pot with lid and bring to a boil over medium-high heat.

3. Reduce to very low heat (water should barely be bubbling) and simmer for 6 hours.

4. At the end of 6 hours, add potatoes and carrots and turn up heat until water simmers again then reduce heat to low, keeping lid on.

5. After 6 hours and 30 minutes add cabbage. Continue simmering with lid on.

6. After 7 hours and the cabbage is tender, use tongs to remove corned beef from the pot. Allow it to rest briefly.

7. Scrape off any fat from corned beef and discard.

8. Slice corned beef at right angles to the grain of the meat and place on serving platter.

9. In one or more separate serving dishes, dish up the cooked vegetables with a slotted spoon. (Cut cabbage into serving-size pieces.)

10. Serve with butter for vegetables.

Enchiladas Rojas

Serves 6. Prep time: 30 minutes, plus 25 minutes for baking.

This crowd-pleasing dish can be made ahead of time up to step 12 (except step 9) below then refrigerated until ready to bake. If you do this, allow pan of enchiladas to come up to room temperature before baking (or bake for a bit longer). Serve this dish with Refried Beans (page 91) and Spanish Rice (page 90).

1 pound Mexican chorizo

1 tablespoon dried chilies or crushed red pepper

1 (8 ounce) can whole tomatoes

1 small yellow onion, diced

1 clove garlic, minced

½ teaspoon iodized salt

3 tablespoons olive oil

½ cup whipping cream

Twelve 6-inch corn tortillas

½ cup shredded mild cheddar cheese, for garnish

¼ cup chopped green onion, for garnish

1. If chorizo sausages are used (rather than bulk sausage), remove the meat from the casings.

2. Brown chorizo in a medium-sized skillet over medium heat. Drain oil and set aside.

3. In a blender, combine chilies, tomatoes, onion, garlic, and salt and blend until smooth.

4. Place blended mixture in a medium skillet with 1 tablespoon olive oil and cook on medium heat while stirring, 3 to 4 minutes.

5. Add whipping cream and stir until combined.

6. Add cooked chorizo and mix. Set aside, but keep warm.

7. In a small skillet over medium heat, add remaining 2 tablespoons olive oil and heat briefly.

8. Place tortillas one at a time in hot oil and cook for 1 minute on each side. Drain on paper towels. (After cooking several tortillas, you may need to add more oil for remaining ones.)

9. Preheat oven to 350 degrees F.

10. Spoon filling (it may be a little runny) into each tortilla, roll, and place each in a greased 9 x 13-inch baking pan until all 12 are completed.

11. Add remaining filling to edges of the baking pan.

12. Cover pan with lid or aluminum foil.

13. Place pan in pre-heated oven and cook for 20 minutes.

14. Remove from oven and sprinkle cheese evenly over top. Return to oven (uncovered) to melt cheese (about 2 minutes).

15. Using a spatula, place 2 enchiladas on each serving plate and sprinkle with green onion.

Grilled Stuffed Peppers

Serves 4 to 6, depending on the size of the pepper. Prep time: about 20 minutes, plus 15 minutes for grilling or baking.

Typically, stuffed bell peppers are oven baked standing in a pan with ½ inch of water, but I prefer the taste of cooking them on a grill. If you want to grill the stuffed peppers, then stand them in a 6-inch (4 peppers) or 8-inch (6 peppers) cast-iron skillet and place the skillet on the grill. Be sure to use an oven mitt to remove skillet from grill as the handle will be hot!

1 pound (80 percent lean) hamburger meat

½ cup chopped yellow onion

½ cup chopped green or red (or both) sweet bell pepper

1 clove garlic, minced

½ teaspoon iodized salt

½ teaspoon ground black pepper

1 teaspoon paprika

½ cup ketchup

4 to 6 whole green bell peppers

½ cup shredded medium cheddar cheese

1. Brown meat on stove over medium heat in a large skillet.

2. Add onions, peppers, and garlic and cook, stirring, for 5 minutes.

3. Add salt, pepper, paprika, and ketchup and stir thoroughly. Set aside.

4. Cut off tops of the whole peppers and remove internal seeds and veins.

5. Spoon hamburger mixture into green pepper cavity, packing it tightly.

6. Top with shredded cheese.

7. If grilling, place stuffed peppers in skillet on heated grill (350 degrees F) and close lid. Cook for 10 minutes or until peppers are cooked and filling is bubbling. If oven baking, preheat to 350 degrees. Place stuffed peppers upright in a baking dish. Add ½ inch of water to dish and bake for 15 minutes or until peppers are cooked and filling is bubbling.

Sloppy Joes

Serves 4. Prep time: about 20 minutes.

This is a great recipe to use when you forgot to take the hamburger out of the freezer on time! I like to serve this with cooked green beans as a side dish. Leftovers can be used to stuff peppers in my Grilled Stuffed Peppers (page 69).

1 pound (80 percent lean) hamburger meat

½ cup chopped yellow onion

½ cup chopped green or red (or both) sweet bell pepper

1 clove garlic, minced

½ teaspoon iodized salt

½ teaspoon ground black pepper

1 teaspoon paprika

½ cup ketchup

4 hamburger buns

1. Brown meat on stove over medium heat in a large skillet.

2. Add onions, peppers, and garlic and cook, stirring, for 5 minutes.

3. Add salt, pepper, paprika, and ketchup and stir thoroughly.

4. Spoon onto hamburger buns and serve closed or open-faced.

Spaghetti with Meat Sauce

Serves 10. Prep time: about 4 hours.

You can make the sauce part of this recipe ahead and refrigerate for 2 days or freeze for later (use within 2 months for best quality).This is one of the most frequently made and popular dishes that I have prepared. Serve with a tossed green salad with salad dressing of your choice or try my Greek Salad (page 27).

1 pound uncooked bulk Italian sausage (if using Italian sausages in casings, cut into ¾-inch-long chunks)

½ cup finely chopped yellow onion

¼ cup minced garlic

4 cups chopped fresh (or frozen, homegrown) peeled tomatoes—or substitute three (16 ounce) cans of canned whole tomatoes, plus 1 teaspoon sugar

1 (6 ounce) can tomato paste

1 (4 ounce) can mushroom stems and pieces, drained

1 (6 ounce) can pitted whole or half black olives, drained (if whole, cut in half)

1 (14 ounce) can beef broth

2 tablespoons fresh minced oregano

1 teaspoon fresh minced thyme

1 teaspoon fresh minced parsley

½ teaspoon crushed red pepper flakes

1 teaspoon celery salt

1 teaspoon iodized salt

1 teaspoon freshly ground black pepper

1 pound whole wheat spaghetti noodles

1 cup grated Parmesan cheese

1. In a large 3-quart deep skillet, Dutch oven, saucepan, or stockpot, crumble and brown sausage over medium heat. Drain fat and return to stove.

2. Reduce heat to low and add onion and garlic to sausage. Stir and cook for 5 minutes, until onion is soft and translucent, but not brown.

3. Add remaining ingredients and stir.

4. Cover pan with lid or aluminum foil and cook on low heat for about 2 hours, stirring occasionally.

5. Remove lid and cook for an additional hour or until mixture thickens to your liking.

6. Cook and drain spaghetti noodles per instructions on package. Portion noodles onto plates or into shallow bowls.

7. Ladle sauce over noodles.

8. Top each serving with grated Parmesan cheese.

Chicken-Fried Steak with Country Gravy

Serves 4. Prep time: about 30 minutes.

This traditional dish is always a hit. I like to serve it with boiled new peeled red potatoes, Pickled Red Beets (page 187), and steamed green beans. Another favorite side serving option replaces pickled red beets with sliced raw marinated onion. To prepare onions, peel and slice (¼-inch-thick) large yellow or red onions and marinate for 10 minutes immersed in apple cider vinegar with salt and pepper. Remove onion slices from the marinade and serve.

4 pieces cube steak (4 to 6 ounces each)

Flouring:

¾ cup all-purpose flour

1 tablespoon cornmeal

1 teaspoon baking powder

½ teaspoon iodized salt

½ teaspoon freshly ground black pepper

¼ teaspoon cayenne pepper

Egg mixture:

1 large egg, beaten

½ cup half-and-half

½ teaspoon fresh lemon juice

1 clove garlic, pressed

Dash of hot sauce (I use Tabasco)

Frying:

½ cup peanut oil

Gravy:

Skillet drippings

¼ cup all-purpose flour

1 cup 2 percent milk, heated

Iodized salt and ground black pepper to taste

1. Preheat oven to 200 degrees F.

2. Combine all flouring ingredients in small shallow dish and set aside.

3. Combine all egg mixture ingredients and mix well in shallow dish.

4. Heat oil until it shimmers in large cast-iron skillet.

5. Coat steak pieces in seasoned flour mixture. Then, one by one, dip them into egg mixture until well coated. Place each piece carefully into hot oil.

6. Fry for about 8 minutes on each side or until both sides are golden brown.

7. Remove meat from skillet and set aside in warm oven.

8. Remove all but about 2 tablespoons of oil from skillet. Do not wash skillet.

9. Add ¼ cup flour to skillet; blend oil and flour over medium heat, stirring to prevent burning mixture.

10. Add milk, plus salt and pepper to taste; stir well.

11. Continue to stir until mixture boils and thickens. Reduce heat.

12. Serve meat on each plate and cover with gravy.

Stuffed Cabbage

Serves 12. Prep time: about 1 hour and 30 minutes.

This dish can be fully prepared ahead of time then refrigerated until ready to bake. I serve stuffed cabbage when I make Coleslaw (Page 26) or Sauerkraut (Page 188) since it provides a use for the cabbage outer leaves which are not used in the coleslaw or sauerkraut.

Cabbage leaves:

12 large outer leaves from heads of green cabbage

1 cup water, for steaming leaves

Stuffing:

⅓ cup brown rice

1 cup water

1½ pounds lean ground beef

1 clove garlic, crushed

1 slice white bread, torn into small pieces

1 large egg, beaten

1 teaspoon Worcestershire sauce

½ teaspoon dried basil

1 teaspoon iodized salt

Sauce:

1 large yellow onion, diced

2 tablespoons butter

1 (15 ounce) can tomato sauce

2 teaspoons hot sauce (I use Tabasco)

1 teaspoon brown sugar

1 teaspoon ground black pepper

Cook cabbage leaves:

1. Bring water to a boil in a large pot. Add cabbage leaves and cover pot with lid.

2. Steam for 1 minute or until leaves become limp.

3. Drain and set aside to cool.

Stuffing:

1. In a small saucepan, add rice and water and cook over medium heat until fluffy, following instructions on rice package. Set aside to cool.

2. While rice is cooking, mix ground beef and other stuffing ingredients together.

3. Add rice to meat mixture and set aside.

Sauce:

1. In large skillet over medium heat, sauté onions in butter until translucent.

2. Add remaining ingredients, stir and cook for 5 minutes.

To assemble:

1. Preheat oven to 325 degrees F.

2. Pour cooked sauce in bottom of a 9 x 13-inch ovenproof baking dish.

3. On your work surface, lay out a cabbage leaf and place ½ cup stuffing in its center.

4. Roll up edge nearest you over the stuffing and tuck in under stuffing. Next, turn the 2 side edges of the leaf into the center and complete the roll by rolling the leaf-covered stuffing away from you until all of the leaf is in the roll.

5. Place stuffed leaf into sauce in baking dish, keeping edge down so it does not unroll.

6. Repeat stuffing and rolling steps until all 12 servings are complete.

7. Place in oven and bake uncovered for 45 minutes.

8. To serve, place a cabbage roll on each plate and ladle on some sauce from baking pan.

Lasagna

Serves 10. Prep time: about 4 hours.

Lasagna is a great dish to serve with a tossed green salad to feed a large crowd. This recipe can be made (up to step 9) a day or two in advance. Just cover lasagna dish(s) with plastic and refrigerate until ready to bake. You can also make the sauce only and freeze for later use (within 2 months). I like to make the lasagna in individual 16-ounce ovenproof single-serving baking dishes because they are easy to serve and look nice on the table. Any size or shape of casserole baking dish or metal baking or loaf pan with 2-inch sides can be used for the lasagna. If you are making the lasagna to take somewhere (like to a potluck), make it in a throwaway aluminum foil pan because there won't be any left over to take home!

Sauce:

1 pound bulk Italian sausage

1 pound lean ground beef

1 finely chopped large yellow onion

2 large cloves garlic, minced

3½ to 4 cups fresh (or frozen, homegrown) cored and peeled tomatoes (substitute 4 cups of canned tomatoes)

1 (6 ounce) can tomato paste

1 (6.5 ounce) can mushroom stems and pieces, drained

1 (6 ounce) can pitted whole or half black olives, drained (If whole, cut in half)

2 tablespoons fresh minced oregano

½ teaspoon fresh minced rosemary

1 teaspoon fresh minced thyme

½ teaspoon fennel seed

¼ teaspoon dried basil

2 teaspoons iodized salt

½ teaspoon freshly ground black pepper

Lasagna noodles:

10 whole wheat lasagna noodles (½ box)

Cheeses:

4 ounces grated Parmesan cheese

1½ pounds grated mozzarella cheese

1 pound ricotta cheese

DAD'S HOME COOKING

1. Over medium heat in a deep 3-quart skillet, Dutch oven, saucepan, or stockpot, crumble and brown sausage with ground beef. Drain fat (if any) and return to stove.

2. Reduce heat to low and add onion and garlic to meats. Stir and cook for 5 minutes, until onion turns translucent but not brown.

3. Add remaining sauce ingredients (up to lasagna noodles) and stir.

4. Cover pan with lid or aluminum foil and cook on low heat for about 2 hours, stirring occasionally.

5. Remove lid and cook for 1 additional hour or until mixture thickens to your liking.

6. Cook noodles in large pot with 4 quarts of boiling water according to package instructions; noodles should be cooked for about 8 minutes and should still be a little underdone. Carefully drain boiling water into sink using a colander to retain noodles. Return noodles to cooking pot and add cold water to rinse and cool the noodles. Drain using the colander and lay them out individually on countertop or cookie sheet so noodles do not stick together.

7. In the baking dish(es) you decide to use (see introduction above), assemble ingredients in the following order: layer of noodles (cut crosswise into shorter pieces if needed), layer of meat sauce, dollops of ricotta, layer of mozzarella, and layer of Parmesan. Repeat.

8. If desired, cover with plastic wrap and refrigerate until ready to bake.

9. Bake in a 350-degree F oven for 30 minutes (add 5 to 10 minutes if lasagna was cold from the refrigerator) until tops are golden brown. Cool for 5 minutes and serve.

Meat Loaf

Serves 6. Prep time: about 2 hours.

Peeled and cut potatoes and carrots can be added alongside the loaf halfway through baking to provide a complete meal. Refrigerate leftovers and reheat in a microwave, or slice and use cold in sandwiches.

2 pounds lean hamburger

1 cup finely chopped yellow onion

1 teaspoon horseradish

1 cup finely chopped celery

1 cup old-fashioned thick rolled oats

1 (4 ounce) can mushroom stems and pieces, drained

2 large eggs, beaten

Half of an 11.5-ounce can of hot and spicy vegetable juice (substitute tomato juice with added hot sauce)

1 teaspoon dry mustard, or prepared mustard, or use my Mustard (page 174)

2 teaspoons iodized salt

2 teaspoons freshly ground black pepper

2 strips bacon, for garnish

Ketchup, for garnish

1. Preheat oven to 350 degrees F.
2. Place all ingredients except bacon and ketchup in large mixer bowl with mixing paddle.
3. Mix well while scraping down sides.
4. Coat a 9 x 13-inch baking dish with olive oil and place mixture in dish.
5. Using your hands, shape meat mixture into a loaf in middle of dish; it should be about 4 inches wide by 4 inches high, the full length of the pan.
6. Place bacon strips on top of loaf.
7. Squirt ribbons on ketchup over top of the loaf.
8. Bake for 1½ hours or until loaf is cooked in middle and top is nicely browned.
9. Remove from oven and let cool 10 minutes before slicing each serving.

Macaroni and Cheese

Serves 8. Prep time: 45 minutes.

Macaroni and cheese is a very common dish that is always enjoyed. This recipe adds a bit of chopped fresh red pepper and thin slices of hot dog to add interest and flavor. If I asked the kids what they wanted for dinner, it was always macaroni and cheese; they loved it!

3 cups elbow macaroni

8 tablespoons (1 stick) butter

1 cup finely chopped yellow onion

½ cup finely chopped red pepper such as pimento or bell

¼ cup all-purpose flour

1¾ cups 2 percent milk

1 pound sharp cheddar cheese, cut into ½-inch cubes

1 hot dog, cut into ⅛-inch slices

1 teaspoon iodized salt

1 teaspoon freshly ground white pepper

6 saltine crackers (2 inches square), crushed, for garnish

1 teaspoon paprika, for garnish

Sauce:

1. Melt butter in a large cast-iron skillet over low to medium heat.

2. Add onion and chopped red pepper, cook, stirring, for 5 minutes.

3. Add flour and mix well.

4. Add milk and stir until mixture thickens and is creamy.

5. Add diced cheese and stir until all cheese is melted.

6. Add hot dog, salt, and pepper.

7. Remove from heat, but keep warm.

Cook macaroni at same time as making sauce:

1. In a large pot, bring 2 quarts water to boil with 1 teaspoon salt and 1 tablespoon olive oil.

2. Add macaroni and cook for about 5 minutes until macaroni is tender.

3. Drain water from macaroni.

Assemble:

1. Preheat oven to 350 degrees F.

2. Add macaroni to sauce and mix thoroughly.

3. Transfer from skillet to a 9 x 13-inch ovenproof casserole dish.

4. Coat top with the crushed crackers and sprinkle with paprika.

5. Place in oven and bake for 20 minutes or until top is golden brown and bubbly.

6. Let cool slightly before serving.

Martha's Hash Brown Casserole

Serves 10. Prep time: 1 hour.

This recipe is from my friend and neighbor Martha Overall. It's easy to make and very tasty.

1 (2 pound) package frozen hash browns

¼ cup margarine or butter, melted

1 (10¾ ounce) can condensed cream of chicken soup

2 cups sour cream

2 cups grated medium cheddar cheese

1 teaspoon iodized salt

1 teaspoon freshly ground white pepper

1. Preheat oven to 350 degrees F.

2. In a large bowl, thoroughly mix all ingredients, breaking up any frozen potatoes.

3. Grease a 9 x 13-inch ovenproof casserole dish.

4. Evenly spread potato mixture in casserole dish.

5. Bake for 45 minutes or until top is lightly browned.

Potatoes Au Gratin

Serves 4. Prep time: 50 minutes for baking potatoes, 1 hour for potatoes to cool, 15 minutes to assemble, and 30 minutes to bake.

This is a good way to use leftover baked potatoes, so when you bake potatoes, bake 2 extra and then make this dish the next day in 45 minutes. Use as side dish for baked ham, beef steak, or pork chops.

2 russet baking potatoes (about 2 pounds)

2 tablespoons butter

2 tablespoons finely chopped yellow onion

1 large clove garlic, minced

2 tablespoons all-purpose flour

1½ cup 2 percent milk, heated

1 cup shredded sharp cheddar cheese

3 tablespoons grated Parmesan cheese

Iodized salt and freshly ground black pepper to taste

½ teaspoon paprika

1. Preheat oven to 450 degrees F.

2. Wash and pat potatoes dry. Puncture potato with fork tines to allow steam to escape. Rub with olive oil.

3. Bake potatoes for 45 minutes or until a fork indicates that potatoes are cooked in center.

4. Let potatoes cool in refrigerator for about 1 hour. (Potatoes can be baked several days in advance and refrigerated if desired.)

5. When potatoes are cool, peel and slice them into ¼-inch rounds.

6. Layer potatoes in buttered 8 x 8-inch ovenproof casserole dish.

7. Preheat oven to 400 degrees F.

8. Make sauce by melting butter in a medium-sized skillet over medium-low heat.

9. Add onion and garlic and sauté until translucent.

10. Add flour and stir until mixture is smooth.

11. Add hot milk, stirring constantly until mixture thickens.

12. Add half of the cheddar and Parmesan cheeses and stir until melted.

13. Season with salt and pepper to taste.

14. Pour sauce over potatoes in casserole dish.

15. Sprinkle top with remaining cheddar and Parmesan cheeses.

16. Dust top with paprika.

17. Place casserole in pre-heated oven and bake for 25 minutes or until golden brown.

18. Remove from oven and let stand for 5 minutes before serving.

Rutabagas Au Gratin

Serves 4. Prep time: 20 minutes for cooking the rutabagas, 1 hour to cool, 15 minutes to assemble, and 30 minutes to bake.

Rutabagas, a vegetable that is at its peak in late fall and winter, are often overlooked as a side dish. After a frost they gain flavor. This side dish is great to serve with pork chops.

4 large rutabagas (about 4 pounds)

2 tablespoons butter

2 tablespoons finely chopped yellow onion

1 large clove garlic, minced

2 tablespoons all-purpose flour

1½ cups hot 2 percent milk

1 cup shredded sharp cheddar cheese

3 tablespoons grated Parmesan cheese

Iodized salt and freshly ground black pepper to taste

½ teaspoon paprika

1. Peel rutabagas and cut into chunks about 2 inches square.

2. Place in large saucepan and cover with water. Boil until just fork tender then drain. Do not overcook. (Rutabagas can be cooked several days in advance, drained, and refrigerated if desired.)

3. When rutabagas are completely cool, slice chunks into ¼-inch-thick slices.

4. Layer rutabagas in buttered 8 x 8-inch ovenproof casserole dish.

5. Preheat oven to 400 degrees F.

6. Make sauce by melting butter in a medium-sized skillet on medium-low heat.

7. Add onion and garlic and sauté until translucent.

8. Add flour and stir until mixture is smooth.

9. Add hot milk, stirring constantly until mixture thickens.

10. Add half of the cheddar and Parmesan cheeses and stir until melted.

11. Season with salt and pepper to taste.

12. Pour sauce over rutabagas in the casserole dish.

13. Sprinkle top with remaining cheddar and Parmesan cheeses. Dust top with paprika.

14. Place casserole dish in pre-heated oven and bake for 25 minutes or until golden brown.

15. Remove from oven and let stand for 5 minutes before serving.

Scalloped Potatoes

Serves 8. Prep time: about 1 hour and 15 minutes.

This is a great side dish for baked ham. The leftovers can be used to make breakfast potatoes by chopping up leftover potatoes and frying them in a skillet with olive oil.

1½ pounds russet potatoes (3 or 4 large), peeled and sliced $^1/_{16}$-inch thick

¾ cup finely chopped yellow onion

3 tablespoons butter

3 tablespoons all-purpose flour

1 teaspoon iodized salt

1 teaspoon freshly ground white pepper

1½ cups 2 percent milk

1. Preheat oven to 375 degrees F.

2. Layer potatoes, onions, butter, flour, salt and pepper in buttered 8 x 8-inch oven-proof casserole dish.

3. Scald milk by heating to 180 degrees F or until top of milk becomes frothy with a slight skin on top. This can be done in a 1-quart glass measuring cup in the microwave if you watch it closely. Do not allow it to boil. If you are using a pot on the stove, heat over low heat while stirring continually to avoid scorching.

4. Pour hot scalded milk over potatoes in casserole dish.

5. Cover dish with a lid or aluminum foil.

6. Place casserole in preheated oven and bake for 45 minutes.

7. Remove lid or foil and return casserole dish to oven for 15 more minutes to brown the top.

8. Remove from oven and let rest for 5 minutes before serving.

Onion Rings

Makes 6 servings of 3 to 4 rings per person. If you want larger servings use 2 onions. Prep time: about 30 minutes.

Onion rings are always delicious and they provide that extra interest as a side to many dishes. They also can be served as an appetizer with Ranch Dressing (page 36).

Batter:

½ cup water

½ cup all-purpose flour

¼ cup cornstarch

1 teaspoon baking soda

1 large egg, beaten

2 teaspoons olive oil

¼ teaspoon iodized salt

Onions:

1 large Ailsa Craig, Walla Walla, or other sweet onion

2 cups refined peanut oil, or enough to provide 2 inches of oil in an electric deep fryer or wok

1. Preheat oven to 200 degrees F.

2. Whisk batter ingredients together and set aside.

3. Peel onion and cut in ¼-inch-thick slices.

4. Separate onion rings and place in a bowl of cold water. Discard center of onion or save for other uses. Let onion rings soak until cooking oil is ready.

5. Heat oil to 360 degrees F.

6. Drain onion rings and place on paper towels.

7. Dip each onion ring into batter. Carefully lower into the hot oil, 3 or 4 at a time.

8. Cook each batch for 2 minutes or until golden brown, turning over if necessary.

9. Remove each batch from the oil, drain, and keep in a 200-degree (F.) oven until all batches are cooked.

10. Serve immediately.

Lazy Boy Baked Beans

Serves 6. Prep time: 10 minutes.

Use this recipe if you do not have hours to make a pot of baked beans from scratch. These are easy to fix and they go well with grilled hamburgers.

1 (28 ounce) can pork and beans

¼ cup dark molasses

1. Place ingredients in a medium saucepan and heat over low to medium heat.

2. Stir until bubbly and serve.

Spanish Rice

Serves 6. Prep time: 40 minutes.

I fix this to go with the Enchiladas Rojas (page 67) and Refried Beans (page 91). It can be made ahead of time, refrigerated for a day or two, and reheated.

¼ pound Mexican chorizo

1 cup long-grain rice

1 tablespoon olive oil

½ cup finely chopped yellow onion

1 medium tomato, peeled, cored, and chopped

1 (14.5 ounce) can chicken broth

½ teaspoon iodized salt

1. If sausages are in casings, remove meat and discard casings.

2. Brown chorizo in a medium skillet. Drain oil and set aside.

3. Cook rice in a medium-sized pot per package directions.

4. Place cooked rice and chorizo in large skillet with olive oil.

5. Add onion, tomato, chicken broth, and salt.

6. Cook over medium heat for about 10 minutes, stirring to prevent sticking. Keep warm until served.

Refried Beans

Makes about 2 quarts. Prep time: 4 hours.

This versatile recipe can be used as a hot or cold bean dip to serve with corn chips or as a refried bean side dish. I use this recipe as a side dish with Enchiladas Rojas (page 67) and Spanish Rice (page 90).

4 cups dry pinto beans

3 quarts water, divided

1 large yellow onion, chopped

4 slices raw bacon, cut into small pieces

1 teaspoon iodized salt

1 teaspoon freshly ground black pepper

1 tablespoon olive oil

1 (4 ounce) can chopped green chilies

1 (10 ounce) can diced tomatoes with green chilies (I prefer Ro-Tel Original brand)

2 jalapeño peppers, seeds and membranes removed, chopped

1. Wash beans and remove dirt, sticks, and cracked/broken beans.

2. Place beans with 1 quart of the water in a large stockpot or Dutch oven. Bring to just boiling then drain water from beans, discarding the water.

3. Return bean pot to medium heat and add remaining 2 quarts of water.

4. Add onion, bacon, salt, and pepper and cook at medium-low heat for 3 hours or until beans are tender.

5. Remove from heat. You can proceed to next step or refrigerate or freeze for later use.

6. Grease a large cast-iron skillet or Dutch oven with olive oil.

7. Add beans, chopped green chilies, diced tomatoes, and jalapeños.

8. Mash with potato masher and cook on low heat until beans thicken, about 30 minutes.

9. Adjust salt if needed.

10. Serve hot. Refried beans can be refrigerated or frozen and reheated for later use.

Fried Rice

Serves 6. Prep time: 20 minutes to precook rice plus 3 days for the rice to be in the refrigerator plus 15 minutes to assemble and fry the rice. Note: Skipping the time in the refrigerator will make the fried rice gluey and not very appetizing.

You will need a pot or rice steamer, plus a large skillet or wok for this recipe. It can be served with Sweet and Sour Pork (page 94) and Chicken Chow Mein (page 59).

1¼ cups long-grain white rice

2 cups water

½ cup diced carrot

½ cup fresh or frozen green peas

4 tablespoons peanut oil, divided

2 large eggs, beaten

1 (14 ounce) can beef broth

2 green onions or 1 small leek

1 clove garlic, thinly sliced

1 teaspoon iodized salt

½ teaspoon ground black pepper

2 tablespoons oyster sauce

2 tablespoons sesame oil

1. Rinse rice in water 3 or 4 times until milky water is mostly gone.

2. Place washed rice in pot with lid or rice cooker; add 2 cups water. On medium heat, steam for 10 to 15 minutes or until water is gone and rice is fluffy.

3. Refrigerate rice uncovered for 3 days.

4. Cook carrots and peas in a pan of boiling water for 3 minutes. Drain. (This step can also be done ahead; refrigerate until needed.)

5. Using large skillet or wok, add 1 tablespoon of peanut oil and heat. Add beaten eggs and cook until done, turning and breaking up as they cook. Remove eggs and set aside.

6. Add remaining 3 tablespoons of oil to skillet or wok and heat to 375 degrees F. Add rice and stir to heat for 1 to 2 minutes.

7. Add cooked peas and carrots, cooked eggs, beef broth, green onions, garlic, salt, pepper, oyster sauce, and sesame oil. Stir-fry for 5 minutes or until beef broth has evaporated.

Sweet and Sour Pork

Serves 2. Prep time: about 40 minutes

You will need a deep fryer for this recipe. The pork pieces in this dish have a definite garlic taste. I crave this dish. You can marinate pork in the refrigerator overnight if you wish.

Toppings:

¼ green bell pepper, cut into ¾-inch pieces

¼ red bell pepper, cut into ¾-inch pieces

1 (8 ounce) can pineapple chunks, drained (juice saved)

8 to 10 chunks of cantaloupe, papaya, peach, nectarine, or mango (¾-inch pieces)

8 to 10 chunks of yellow onion (¾-inch pieces of onion layer)

Marinated pork:

1½ pounds pork loin chops or other lean pork cut

¼ cup soy sauce

1 clove garlic, crushed

Sauce:

2 tablespoons brown sugar

4 teaspoons cornstarch

3 tablespoons apple cider vinegar

2 tablespoons soy sauce

Pineapple juice from one 8-ounce can pineapple chunks

2 tablespoons ketchup

1 teaspoon Worcestershire sauce

Batter:

¼ cup water

¼ cup all-purpose flour

2 tablespoons cornstarch

½ teaspoon baking soda

½ large egg, beaten

1 teaspoon olive oil

⅛ teaspoon iodized salt

Deep-frying:

2 cups refined peanut oil or enough to provide 2 inches of oil in electric deep fryer

1 tablespoon raw sesame seeds, for garnish

1. Prepare topping items and set aside.

2. Remove fat from pork; cut from bone and into ¾-inch cubes. Place cubes in a small bowl containing the marinade of soy sauce and garlic. Set aside. Discard fat and bone.

3. Prepare sauce by combining ingredients in a small saucepan. Cook over medium heat, stirring until combined. Continue to cook until sauce thickens. Reduce heat to low to just keep the sauce warm. (If sauce becomes too thick, thin with water.)

4. Add peanut oil to electric deep fryer and preheat to 375 degrees F.

5. Whisk batter ingredients in a small bowl.

6. Drain marinade from pork and discard.

7. Dip pork pieces 6 to 8 at a time into batter.

8. Place basket into deep fryer. Remove battered pork pieces one at a time from batter and carefully drop into hot oil, being careful not to splash. Repeat until all 6 to 8 pieces are in the oil. *Note: Adjust the number of pieces you deep fry at a time to accommodate your fryer size.*

9. Cook for about 5 minutes or until golden brown, stirring and separating pieces if necessary.

10. Remove fry basket from oil and drain pork on paper towel.

11. Repeat steps 7 through 10 until all pork pieces are cooked.

12. Briefly warm topping ingredients by tossing them in a lightly oiled hot skillet or wok; add sauce and stir to mix.

13. Place pork in serving dish and pour warmed topping ingredients over pork.

14. Sprinkle with sesame seeds and serve immediately.

Pizza Dough

Makes four 14-inch pizza crusts or two 14-inch crusts and a batch of breadsticks. Note: The pizza recipe that follows is for two 14-inch pizzas, so if you are going to make only 2 pizzas, then either make the bread sticks or freeze half of the dough for later use. Prep time: 10 minutes plus ½ hour rest and minimum 12 hours in refrigerator.

When you are ready to make the pizza, remove dough from the refrigerator and allow it to set for 30 minutes to return to room temperature before rolling out. The pizza dough should be made the day before you want to actually make, bake, and serve the pizza. The refrigerator time is actually a cold rising period that improves the dough's texture and allows it to absorb the garlic flavor. You can keep dough in the refrigerator for 3 or 4 days or freeze it for later use (within 3 months).

1¾ cups lukewarm (80 to 90 degree F) water

1 (0.25 ounce) packet active dry yeast (2½ teaspoons)

⅛ cup yellow cornmeal

1 tablespoon sea salt

2 tablespoons olive oil

1 clove garlic, crushed

1 tablespoon fresh rosemary, minced

4½ cups all-purpose flour, plus extra for dusting work surface

1. Put lukewarm water in electric stand mixer bowl (or an 8-inch bowl if you are mixing by hand). Sprinkle yeast over it, and let stand for 5 minutes or until the yeast has dissolved.

2. Install dough hook in the electric mixer and mix in cornmeal, salt, oil, garlic, and rosemary at low speed (or mix by hand using a wooden spoon).

3. Sift flour. Add 1 cup of sifted flour and mix thoroughly.

4. Add second and third cups of flour and mix well.

5. Add remaining 1½ cup of flour; mix until combined. Transfer dough to floured work surface and briefly knead by hand until dough is smooth.

6. Let dough rest for ½ hour in bowl at room temperature.

7. Separate dough into 4 balls (one for each pizza) of equal size. Wrap each ball in plastic wrap that has been oiled and place in refrigerator for 12 hours.

8. To make pizza crusts or "skins," remove the balls from the refrigerator and allow them to sit at room temperature for 30 minutes. Prepare the area that you will use to roll out dough by cleaning and drying the countertop or breadboard. Dust rolling surface and rolling pin with flour. Remove plastic wrap from dough balls and flour. Roll each one into increasingly larger circles, using more flour as needed to prevent sticking. Roll and turn skin over to keep well-floured; ultimately, dough will be quite thin—about ⅛-inch thick. The dough is very elastic and will try to shrink as you roll it out, so let it shrink a bit and then roll again. Roll the crust larger than the pan you are using to allow enough crust to fold over and form a raised edge. *Note: If you want to "toss" the skin instead of rolling, be prepared to get flour all over the kitchen, as this is a messy process requiring lots of cleanup. If you still want to try this technique despite the mess, first roll or pull the dough into an 8- to 10-inch round about ½-inch thick and then proceed with the tossing to increase the dough size.*

The dough is now ready for use in the pizza recipe that follows.

Pizza

Makes two 14-inch pies. Prep time: about 1 hour

See Pizza Dough recipe (page 96) for preparing the dough that is used in this recipe. You will need two 14-inch pizza pans for this recipe. This is the most popular dish that I serve. Feel free to change the toppings to your liking.

Sauce: (Make ahead of time by combining all ingredients and refrigerating.)

1 (8 ounce) can tomato sauce

1 (6 ounce) can tomato paste

2 cloves garlic, crushed

2 tablespoons fresh minced or dried oregano

1 teaspoon fresh minced or dried basil

1 teaspoon fresh minced or dried parsley flakes

1 tablespoon crushed red pepper flakes

1 teaspoon sea salt

1 teaspoon ground black pepper

Cheeses: (Make ahead of time and refrigerate. You can also use 4 cups of packaged shredded Italian cheese mix.)

2 cups shredded mozzarella

1 cup shredded mild cheddar

1 cup shredded provolone

Toppings:

3½ ounces sliced pepperoni

½ pound raw Italian sausage

2 (4 ounce) cans mushrooms, stem and pieces, drained

1 (15 ounce) can pitted black olives, cut in half

½ cup shredded Parmesan cheese

1. Preheat oven to 450 degrees F with racks in the mid area of the oven or prepare a wood-fired oven to 500 degrees.

2. Coat pizza pans with olive oil to prevent sticking, and place pizza dough skins onto pans, pinching edges to provide an upturned crust at the edges.

3. Place half of the sauce onto each skin and spread evenly, to within ½ inch of the edge.

4. Sprinkle half of the cheeses evenly over tomato sauce, also to within ½ inch of the pan edge.

5. Place half of the pepperoni in each pan, dealing out the slices evenly.

6. Divide sausage in ½ for each pie and distribute teaspoon-sized pieces evenly on each pie.

7. Spread 1 can of drained mushrooms evenly on each pie.

8. Spread ½ can of the cut olives evenly on each pie.

9. Top each pie with Parmesan cheese and spread evenly.

10. Place pizza pans in oven, one on each rack, and cook about 40 minutes until crust bottom is brown and toppings are cooked. *Note: Switch pan positions in the oven halfway through baking period. (It will take less time in the wood-fired oven, so watch pies carefully to avoid burning them.)*

11. Remove from oven, let cool for 2 minutes, and then slice each pie into 8 pieces and serve.

Fish and Chips

Serves 6. Prep time: about 1½ hours.

The chips can be prepared up to last fry and frozen for use later. See Tartar Sauce (page 177) for the classic accompaniment. You will need a deep fryer or Dutch oven for this recipe.

Chips:

4 pounds russet potatoes (about 8 medium)

½ cup cider vinegar

1 tablespoon iodized salt

Fish:

18 pieces (about 3 pounds) ling cod, sea bass, rock fish, or other white-meat fish

¼ cup cornstarch

Batter:

1 cup all-purpose flour

1 tablespoon cornmeal

1½ teaspoon baking powder

½ teaspoon iodized salt

½ teaspoon celery salt

½ teaspoon dry mustard

½ teaspoon ground black pepper

¼ teaspoon paprika

¼ teaspoon ground celery seeds

¼ teaspoon ground bay leaves

¼ teaspoon cayenne pepper

⅛ teaspoon ground nutmeg

⅛ teaspoon ground ginger

Pinch of ground cloves, mace, allspice, and cinnamon

1 bottle lager beer (you may use less than the full bottle)

1 quart refined peanut oil for deep frying (or enough oil to yield 2 inches of oil in your fryer)

1. Whisk batter ingredients in small bowl and set aside; add beer until mixture has consistency of paint.

2. Wash potatoes. Peel if desired, and slice into long strips, ¼-inch square. Place in large bowl filled with cold water.

3. In large pot over high heat, bring 1 gallon water with vinegar and salt to 170 degrees F. Reduce heat to maintain temperature. Add drained potatoes and blanch for 20 minutes. Remove potatoes from hot water and dry, using a salad spinner.

4. Preheat oil in a deep fryer or Dutch oven to 365 degrees.

5. Preheat oven to 200 degrees.

6. Using rubber gloves to protect your hands, carefully drop 2 handfuls of potatoes into hot oil and cook for 1 minute being careful not to splash oil.

7. Remove chips from oil using a slotted spoon and drain on paper towels. Repeat steps 6 and 7 until all potatoes are cooked and drained. (Chips can be frozen at this point for later use.) If you are proceeding to finish the chips, let cool to room temperature and set aside.

8. Reduce oil temperature to 350 degrees.

9. Lightly dredge 6 pieces of fish in cornstarch.

10. Dip each fish piece into batter and, again using rubber gloves, lower the 6 pieces of fish into hot oil and cook for 3 to 5 minutes, turning once, until golden brown.

11. Using a slotted spoon, remove fish pieces from oil and drain on paper towels, then move into 200-degree oven. Repeat steps 9 through 11 until all 18 pieces of fish are cooked.

12. Raise oil temperature to 375 degrees. Using rubber gloves to protect your hands, carefully drop 2 handfuls of chips into hot oil and cook for 3 to 4 minutes or until lightly golden brown.

13. Remove chips from oil using a slotted spoon and drain on paper towels. Repeat steps 12 and 13 until all chips are cooked and drained. Keep warm in oven.

14. When all chips are fried, divide chips into 6 servings and place 3 pieces of fish over chips. Serve immediately.

Baked Ham

Serves 12 plus leftovers, and provides ham bones for soup and bean dishes.
Prep time: 4½ hours.

Serve with Scalloped Potatoes (page 87). I generally serve this at Easter but it is always popular, even on a hot summer day when I serve it outside on the deck with steamed green beans and corn on the cob from the garden.

1 (15 to 23 pound) fully cooked bone-in whole ham (I prefer Falls Brand from Independent Meat Company, Twin Falls, Idaho)

1 cup water

1 (10 ounce) can crushed pineapple

¼ cup brown sugar

1 tablespoon prepared mustard

10 whole cloves

1. Preheat oven to 325 degrees F.

2. Remove wrapping from ham and place in large roasting pan with the fat side up.

3. Add water to pan.

4. Strain the can of pineapple and pour liquid into roasting pan.

5. Mix drained pineapple, brown sugar, and mustard; spread evenly onto ham.

6. Stick cloves into top surface of ham and cover with roasting pan lid or aluminum foil.

7. Bake for 4 hours (15 minutes per pound) or until a meat thermometer reads 160 degrees when inserted deep into the ham, but not touching the bone.

8. Remove from oven, remove cloves, and cool for at least 15 minutes before carving.

9. Leftovers can be frozen for additional meals; use within 2 months. To prepare leftovers, cut remaining ham slices off ham and package for freezing. Remove remaining ham from bone, dice and package for freezing for use in dishes like scrambled eggs. Finally, cut bone into 2 or 3 pieces (using a meat saw or a clean metal hacksaw) and freeze for use in soup or bean dishes.

Beef Rib Roast Au Jus

Serves 8. Prep time: about 3 hours.

Since it's an expensive cut of beef, I usually save rib roast for special occasions. Serve when the grocery store meat market has rib roasts on sale. If you have room in your freezer, buy one for later use within 3 to 4 months. Serve with Horseradish Sauce (page 173) and York-shire Pudding (page 161). A baked potato with toppings and steamed broccoli or aspara-gus completes the meal. Use a meat thermometer to determine when the roast is done: the internal temperature should be 140 degrees F for rare, 160 degrees for medium, and 170 degrees for well done. Since the meat will continue to cook after it is removed from the oven, you should take the meat from the oven when it reaches 130 degrees for rare, 150 degrees for medium, and 160 degrees for well done. Often you will not know how every dinner guest will want their meat cooked, so I always take the meat out of the oven at 130 degrees to be sure that some rare meat will be available. The end cuts will serve as well done or medium. It takes about 20 minutes per pound to cook to the 130 degree temperature—so an 8-pound roast should be in the 325 degree oven for about 2 hours and 40 minutes. If you are roasting a smaller or larger roast, the time per pound may vary, so check the temperature as it cooks to avoid overcooking.

There will likely be leftovers, including the bones. Refrigerate them within 1 hour after serv-ing. The meat makes delicious sandwiches, hot or cold. The bones and the jus can be boiled for 2 hours in a large pot with additional water. Remove from heat, let cool, and remove any remaining meat from the bones and add the meat bits back into the broth. Discard the bones and freeze the broth for later use (2 months maximum) as a base for vegetable soup, bean soup, pot roast, or other dishes requiring broth.

1 (8 pound) bone-in rib roast

1 tablespoon coarse rock salt

5 cups water, divided

1 (1 ounce) package au jus gravy mix

1. Preheat oven to 325 degrees F.

2. In large stainless steel or porcelain enamel roasting pan that will contain the roast, place roast with fat side up.

3. Rub salt into fat on top of roast.

4. Place uncovered roast in preheated oven; cook for about 2 hours and 40 minutes or until the internal temperature is 130 degrees.

5. Transfer roast to a serving platter. Tent with aluminum foil to keep warm, and allow to rest for 20 minutes before carving.

6. Meanwhile, skim excess fat from drippings in the roasting pan and discard or save if you are making Yorkshire Pudding (page 161).

7. Place roasting pan on the stove over medium heat, add 2 cups of water, and bring to a boil.

8. Stir with a wooden spoon, loosening all the brown bits until they are dissolved.

9. In a small bowl, stir au jus mix with 3 cups cold water until it is dissolved.

10. Add to roasting pan and cook, stirring, until liquid returns to a boil.

11. Carve roast and serve. Ladle the jus into individual 5- to 6-ounce custard cups or ramekins and serve.

Pot Roast

Serves 6. Prep time: about 3 ½ hours.

This recipe uses rutabagas; you can substitute turnips if you like or leave them out. This is a complete meal dish and is great with freshly baked bread or rolls for dipping into the gravy.

2 pounds chuck beef roast

1 large yellow onion, finely chopped

4 cloves garlic, crushed

¼ cup Worcestershire sauce

¼ cup ketchup

2 (14.5 ounce) cans beef broth

1 teaspoon iodized salt

1 teaspoon ground black pepper

1 teaspoon crushed red pepper flakes

1 Roma tomato, cut into pieces

1 stalk celery, cut into ¼-inch slices

6 medium carrots, scraped or peeled and cut into chunks

4 large potatoes, peeled and cut into chunks

3 medium-sized rutabagas, peeled and cut into chunks

2 tablespoons butter

½ cup half-and-half

½ cup all-purpose flour

1 cup cold water

½ cup chopped fresh parsley, for garnish

1. Brown meat in large pot or Dutch oven over medium heat.

2. Add onions and garlic and cook for 5 minutes, stirring.

3. Add remaining ingredients (up to carrots) and bring to a boil.

4. Reduce heat to low and simmer, covered, for 2½ hours, stirring occasionally.

5. Add carrots, potatoes, and rutabagas; turn up heat to bring to a boil.

6. Reduce heat to simmer and cook for about 35 minutes or until vegetables are tender.

7. Using a slotted spoon, remove potatoes and rutabagas; mash together, using a potato masher.

8. Add butter and half-and-half and stir to combine. Set aside in a warm place.

9. Whisk flour with cold water until smooth.

10. Remove meat and carrots from Dutch oven and set aside. Pour flour and water into remaining liquid in the Dutch oven, stirring to thicken gravy.

11. Cook for 5 minutes.

12. To serve, place scoop of potatoes/rutabagas on each serving plate and cover with gravy.

13. Add a serving of meat and carrots to each plate.

14. Garnish with parsley.

Turkey with Dressing and Gravy

Serves 20. Prep time: 8 hours on serving day plus preparing time over the week before serving as described below.

This is a main course dish for Thanksgiving. It can also be served for Christmas, New Year's Eve, Easter, or other special occasions. When whole turkey is on sale, it is by far the least expensive meat you can buy. If you find turkeys on sale (frozen are less expensive than fresh) and if have room in your freezer, buy two; freeze one for later use (within 3 to 4 months).

Should you buy fresh or frozen turkeys? All turkeys you buy in the stores are flash frozen, but those that are sold "fresh" are stopped short of freezing solid, so the choice is yours. Buying a fresh turkey two weeks before you will cook it and not freezing it is pushing the limit; the meat may spoil in the refrigerator. I have cooked many delicious frozen turkeys. Keep them frozen until 4 days before cooking then transfer to the refrigerator until ready to cook (they'll thaw slowly that way, which is ideal for the best finished product). You will need a large roasting pan with a cover (make sure it will fit in your oven) or buy an aluminum foil roasting pan and cover with aluminum foil. I roast mine in the outdoor barbeque, since it has the capability to add smoking and it has a temperature gauge, allowing the roasting temperature to be carefully maintained.

Leftovers are likely (be sure and refrigerate them within 1 hour after serving) and can provide great meals, including turkey noodle soup, turkey à la king, and hot or cold turkey sandwiches. Once most of the meat is removed from the carcass, you can either freeze it for later processing (it will keep for up to 1 month) or make turkey stock by placing the carcass in a large pot with water to cover. Bring to a boil, reduce heat, and allow to simmer for 1 to 2 hours. Let cool, remove large bones, and discard them. Place pot in the refrigerator and let stock cool until the fat gels on the top. Skim and discard the gelled fat. Pour pot contents through a fine sieve to separate bones and meat from broth, saving both. Carefully remove meat from bones and add meat back to broth. Discard bones. Freeze broth and meat for later use in making turkey noodle soup, turkey gravy, or as a substitute for chicken broth.

1 whole turkey, 20 to 22 pounds

1 batch Cornbread (page 150)

1 loaf French bread

1 loaf whole wheat bread

1 large yellow onion, peeled and diced

4 cloves garlic, minced

1 celeriac (celery root), peeled and diced

2 cups chopped celery heart

6 (14.5 ounce) cans chicken broth (You may not use all of these.)

½ pound salted butter (2 cubes), divided

2 large eggs, beaten

2 tablespoons poultry seasoning

2 tablespoons minced fresh or ground sage

2 tablespoons iodized salt

2 tablespoons ground black pepper

2 cups semi-dry white wine (Gewurztraminer or Liebfraumilch, or substitute nonalcoholic apple cider)

1 cup all-purpose flour (You may not use all of this.)

One week before your dinner:

1. Make cornbread and cool.

2. Dice cornbread into ½-inch cubes and place in large bowl.

3. Cube loaves of French and whole wheat bread; add to bowl. Cubes should be ¾ inch or less in size.

4. Throughout the week, stir bread pieces to allow all to dry. They should not be allowed to mold, so dry quickly and thoroughly. *Note: If you live in a high humidity area, you may need to dry the breads in your oven at low temperature or use a food dehydrator.*

Four days before your dinner:

1. If turkey is frozen, remove from freezer and refrigerate.

2. If you are using a fresh turkey, put in refrigerator.

MAIN DISHES

One day before your dinner:

1. Calculate when you want your turkey ready to serve. Assuming you want to serve your meal at 4:00 p.m., your turkey needs to be done and out of the oven by 3:00 p.m.

2. A 20- to 22-pound turkey, stuffed, will take 5 to 6 hours (convection ovens take less time) to cook at 325 degrees F (meat thermometer reading 180 to 185 degrees), so the turkey must be stuffed and in the preheated oven by 9:00 a.m.

3. This means that you need to start preparing the turkey and dressing at 8:00 a.m. on the day you want to serve.

Beginning at 8:00 a.m. on the day of your dinner:

1. Remove turkey from refrigerator and place in a well-cleaned sink.

2. Remove plastic wrapping and metal or plastic wires (the ones that hold legs to carcass) from turkey.

3. Remove neck and giblets (heart, liver, and gizzard) from neck and body cavities. Set aside.

4. Wash carcass inside and out with cold water, drain, and set in roasting pan breast side up, with wings folded under the back. Set aside.

5. Wash neck and giblets and place in large pot. (Disinfect sink after this step.)

6. Add onion, garlic, celeriac, celery heart, and 2 cans of chicken broth to pot.

7. Bring to a boil on the stove and cook over medium heat for 30 minutes.

8. Remove neck and giblets from pot and cool until meat can be handled.

9. Finely dice heart and liver and add back to vegetables and liquid in pot.

10. Cut the gizzard in ⅛-inch-thick slices and cut off and discard the outer "skin." Finely dice remaining center meat and add to pot.

11. Remove some meat from the neck (as best as you can) and add to pot. Discard neck bone.

12. Melt one cube of butter and add to pot.

13. Place the dried, assorted bread cubes in a large mixing bowl.

14. 14. Pour hot mixture from pot over bread.

15. 15. Add beaten eggs, spices, and 1 cup of wine; stir mixture until it is well mixed and all the bread is moistened.

16. 16. Preheat oven to 325 degrees F.

17. 17. Stuff dressing into both neck and body cavities of the turkey. Do not pack the dressing too tightly.

18. 18. Place any excess dressing around the edge of turkey.

19. 19. Smear outside of turkey with 2 tablespoons butter and cover.

20. 20. Place turkey in preheated oven and cook for 4 hours, covered with roaster lid or aluminum foil wrapped over top of the turkey and tucked into roasting pan lip.

21. 21. At 4 hours, remove cover, baste turkey with liquid from pan, and return to oven uncovered.

22. 22. At 5 hours, check turkey for brownness and, using a meat thermometer, check temperature at thickest part of thigh. It should be approaching 180 degrees. If it needs to cook more, return to oven and continue roasting.

23. 23. At 5½ hours, check brownness and temperature again. If temperature has reached 180 to 195 degrees, remove turkey from oven.

24. 24. Carefully drain liquid from roasting pan into a bowl. Strain through a sieve then pour into a large pot (the amount of liquid will vary). This liquid broth will be used to make gravy (see below). Cover roasted turkey with its cover and allow to rest in a warm place until ready to carve.

Make gravy:

1. Measure amount of broth that was removed from roaster and pour it back into large pot.

2. Add remaining 1 cup of wine and remaining 6 tablespoons butter.

3. Add enough cans of chicken broth to make a total of 6 cups including turkey broth and wine.

4. Bring to a boil over medium heat.

5. In a small bowl, mix flour with enough cold water to make a thin paste.

6. Slowly add about half of flour/water mixture to boiling broth, stirring until mixture thickens. (If lumps form, dissolve them by whisking or remove using a strainer.)

7. Add more flour/water mixture if gravy is too thin, or add more chicken broth if gravy is too thick.

8. Taste and add salt and pepper if needed.

9. Keep gravy warm over low heat until ready to serve.

10. To serve, pour gravy into gravy boat.

To carve the turkey:

1. Using a large spoon, remove enough stuffing to fill serving dish.

2. Using a sharp carving knife and fork, carve turkey meat and place on a warmed serving platter, placing dark meat on one side and white meat on the other. (Carve breast meat down and parallel to breastbone, removing slices about ¼-inch thick. Remove meat from thighs and wings by using a knife or fork to strip meat.)

3. Keep turkey platter warm until it is served.

Desserts

Many cookbooks have lots of dessert recipes. Some are difficult and time consuming to make. I once made a frozen ice cream log from a recipe out of *Bon Appetit* magazine that took forever to make. That was enough for me. I gave up making cakes from scratch years ago, because packaged cake mixes and icings you can buy today are very good, very easy to make, and often on sale. Some are even sugar free! Thus, in our household, birthday cakes were always from mixes, and the kids would always get to choose their favorite cake type (German chocolate was the favorite). The only cake recipe I've included in this cookbook is a chocolate-mayonnaise sheet cake recipe that my mother made when I was a kid. It was my favorite.

Purchased pies and pie crust are a different story—with few exceptions, the ones you buy aren't tasty or worth what they cost. Pies are my favorite dessert, and the only way to get a good pie is to make the crust and filling from scratch. I have included mostly fruit pies in this book. But by starting with a baked pie shell (see Pie Crust, page 114), you can, after cooling the shell, fill it with your favorite pudding, then top with whipped cream. Dry, prepackaged instant pudding fillings, either with or without sugar and fat free, make wonderful cream pies such as butterscotch, lemon (add lemon zest), chocolate, pistachio, and banana cream (add a real banana). Use two boxes of pudding mix (1.4 ounces each) and 2¾ cups of 2 percent milk for each nine-inch pie.

Cookie recipes are also found in abundance on the Internet or in cookbooks, so try those out, as most are easy to make. I have only included one popular cookie recipe in this book. The kids liked these and I enjoy them to this day. I am not a candy eater or maker, so no candy recipes are included.

Pie Crust

Makes one 9½-inch double pie crust. Prep time: 15 minutes, plus 30 minutes rest time.

This recipe can be made ahead of time and refrigerated for up to one week. I often double the recipe and refrigerate half for use the next week. I use this crust for all of my pie recipes.

2 cups all-purpose flour (plus extra for rolling dough)

½ teaspoon iodized salt

½ teaspoon baking powder

⅞ cup of vegetable shortening that has been chilled in the refrigerator

⅛ cup water

½ teaspoon white vinegar

1 large, egg, beaten

1. Sift flour, salt, and baking powder together in 8-inch bowl.

2. Add shortening and cut in with a pastry cutter until mixture looks flakey.

3. Combine water, vinegar, and about half the beaten egg and add to flour mixture. (Save and use other half of egg for glazing the top crust.)

4. Mix with pastry cutter until dough is formed.

5. Form dough into a ball and wrap in plastic wrap. Let rest for 30 minutes before rolling out or refrigerate for later, allowing time to let dough return to room temperature before rolling out.

Variation: To make two single, prebaked pie shells for cream pies, divide the ball of dough in half and roll out (See Apple Pie, page 115, steps 3 through 6, for more information on rolling). Lay shells into 2 pie pans. Prick the bottom of the pie shells with a fork about 30 times (this allows the steam to escape). Chill the shells for 15 minutes then bake shells in a 425-degree F, preheated oven for 12 minutes, or until lightly browned. Allow to cool before filling.

Apple Pie

*Makes one 9½-inch deep-dish pie. Prep time: about 1½ hours,
if dough is made ahead of time.*

Serve with a scoop of vanilla ice cream. I generally serve apple pie in fall and winter when fresh apples are available. It is also a hit on Fourth of July and Labor Day.

8 to 10 (6 to 8 ounce) Granny Smith, Jonathan, or other tart apples (about 5 pounds)

¾ cup sugar or sugar substitute (I use either Splenda or stevia), plus 1 tablespoon to sprinkle on top

1 heaping tablespoon all-purpose flour, plus more for rolling

½ teaspoon iodized salt

¼ teaspoon ground cinnamon

Dash of ground nutmeg

1 tablespoon butter

Half of beaten egg saved from pie dough. (See Pie Crust, Page 114.)

1. Preheat oven to 425 degrees F.

2. Peel apples then slice into quarters and remove core. Slice quarters in half lengthwise then cut those slices into ¼-inch-thick pieces. Put apples in 8-inch bowl. You should have 10 cups of apple chunks. Mix all ingredients (except butter and beaten egg) with apples in bowl and set aside.

3. If dough has been refrigerated, allow to warm to room temperature. Unwrap the dough and divide it into two balls: ⅔ (bottom crust) and ⅓ (top crust).

4. Dust clean countertop, pastry board, plastic wrap, or cloth with flour; place larger ball on dusted surface and flatten into a disk.

5. Roll out dough with a flour-dusted rolling pin, keeping both sides of the dough dusted with flour by turning flattened dough over with a spatula. If edges split, repair. Roll from center out until dough is about 12 inches in diameter and ⅛-inch thick.

6. Carefully roll dough onto rolling pin and position it over glass pie pan. Unroll dough into pie pan and, using a ½-cup measuring cup, smooth out dough to

conform to pan. Patch any holes or splits. Remove excess dough around edge and add to remaining dough ball.

7. Fill pan with apple mixture and pat down top to a dome. *Note: Apples will cook down, so center of dome can be 2 inches above pan edge. Pie, when cooked, will be flat or slightly concave.*

8. Dot butter over apple mixture.

9. Roll out top crust ball, following step 5 above. The finished dough circle will be about 10 inches in diameter and ⅛-inch thick.

10. Place rolled-out dough on top of apple mixture, using rolling pin as in step 6.

11. Seal top to bottom crust at edge; remove and discard any excess dough.

12. With a small knife, cut 8 to10 small slits in top crust to allow steam to escape when baking.

13. Using a pastry brush, brush top crust with beaten egg leftover from pie dough recipe.

14. Sprinkle top crust with 1 tablespoon sugar.

15. Bake for about 40 minutes or until top is nicely browned and filling is bubbly.

16. Remove and allow pie to partially cool before serving.

Pumpkin Pie

Serves 16 (two pies). Prep time: 1½ hours.

This pie can be made a day ahead and refrigerated, covered tightly. If you do refrigerate, allow pie to return to room temperature before baking. This pie is traditional for Thanksgiving dinner. It is a variation of the Libby's pumpkin pie recipe found on their cans of pumpkin.

Pie Crust (page 114)

1 (29 ounce) can solid-pack pumpkin (I prefer Libby's) or 3⅝ cups of cooked winter squash or pumpkin, strained to remove any stringy pulp

4 large eggs, slightly beaten

1 cup sugar or sugar substitute (I use Splenda or stevia)

2 teaspoons ground cinnamon

1 teaspoon ground ginger

½ teaspoon ground cloves

½ teaspoon iodized salt

2 (12 ounce) cans evaporated whole milk

About 4 cups whipped cream or purchased whipped topping

Mint sprigs, for garnish

1. Preheat oven to 425 degrees F.

2. Divide pie dough in half and roll out each pie crust (see Apple Pie, page 115, steps 4 through 6) and place in 9½-inch glass pie pans.

3. Combine remaining ingredients (except whipped cream topping) and mix well.

4. Pour pumpkin mixture into pie shells.

5. Bake for 15 minutes. Reduce oven setting to 350 degrees and continue to bake for an additional 40 to 50 minutes or until a toothpick inserted in center comes out clean.

6. Allow to cool; top each serving with a dollop of whipped cream and a mint sprig.

Grapefruit Pie

Serves 8. Prep time: 1 hour, plus 1 to 2 hours refrigeration time.

This pie can be made a day ahead and refrigerated. It is very refreshing and is great to serve on a hot day—or as dessert after a spicy main-course dinner.

1 (9½-inch) prebaked pie shell (see Pie Crust, page 114, "Variation")

1 (15 ounce) can grapefruit sections

30 large white marshmallows

1 cup heavy cream, whipped

Mint sprigs, for garnish

1. Drain liquid off grapefruit and reserve ½ cup.

2. In a pan over medium to low heat, add ½ cup grapefruit juice and marshmallows.

3. Stir constantly until all marshmallows are melted.

4. Cool pan ingredients by setting pan in a shallow bowl of ice water.

5. When mixture starts to thicken, fold in grapefruit sections and whipped cream.

6. Pour mixture into baked, cooled pie crust shell.

7. Refrigerate until mixture is firm, 1 to 2 hours.

8. Cut into slices and serve with a sprig of mint.

Blackberry Pie for a Crowd

Serves 12. Prep time: about 1½ hours, assuming dough is made ahead of time.

Serve with a scoop of vanilla ice cream. You can use fresh or frozen blackberries for this recipe. If berries are frozen, then allow them to thaw before using. If you buy the frozen berries in the store, chances are they were frozen with sugar added. If this is the case, reduce or eliminate the sugar in this recipe.

10 cups blackberries, washed, stems removed

1¾ cups sugar or sugar substitute (I use Splenda or stevia), plus 1 tablespoon to sprinkle on top

½ cup cornstarch

½ teaspoon iodized salt

2 tablespoons fresh lemon juice

Pie dough, doubled from Pie Crust (page 114)

¼ cup all-purpose flour, for dusting work surface

Half of beaten egg saved from Pie Crust (page 114)

1. Preheat oven to 450 degrees F.

2. Mix blackberries, sugar, cornstarch, salt, and lemon juice in 8-inch bowl and set aside.

3. If pie dough has been in the refrigerator, remove it from refrigerator and allow to warm to room temperature. Unwrap and divide into two portions: ⅔ (bottom crust) and ⅓ (top crust).

4. Dust your clean countertop, pastry board, plastic wrap, or cloth with flour; place larger ball on dusted surface and flatten it into a rough square.

5. Roll out dough with a flour-dusted rolling pin, keeping both sides of the dough dusted with flour by turning the flattened dough over with a spatula. If edges split, repair. Roll from the center out until dough is about 14 inches long, 9 inches wide, and ⅛-inch thick.

6. Carefully roll dough onto rolling pin and position over a 7 x 11-inch glass pan. Unroll dough into pie pan and using a ½ cup measuring cup, smooth out dough

to conform to pan. Patch any holes or splits. Remove any excess dough around edge and add to remaining dough ball.

7. Fill pan with blackberry mixture.

8. Roll out top crust, following step 5 above (except dough will be about 8 x 12 inches, and ⅛-inch thick).

9. Place rolled out top dough on top of blackberry mixture using rolling pin, as in step 6 and seal top crust to bottom crust at edges.

10. Using a pastry brush, brush top crust with beaten egg. With a small knife, cut 8 to 10 small slits in top crust to allow steam to escape when baking.

11. Sprinkle top crust with 1 tablespoon sugar.

12. Bake in 450 degree oven for 10 minutes. Reduce temperature to 375 degrees and bake for 40 minutes or until top crust is browned and filling is bubbly.

13. Allow to partially cool before serving.

Peach Pie for a Crowd

Serves 12. Prep time: about 1½ hours, assuming dough is made ahead of time.

You can use this recipe to make apricot or nectarine pie also: Use about 30 ripe apricots or 18 small, ripe nectarines in lieu of peaches. Wash, quarter, and remove pits. Peels can be left on apricots or nectarines. Serve with scoop of vanilla ice cream. You can also use frozen peaches for this recipe. If peaches are frozen, allow them to thaw before using. If you buy frozen peaches in the store, chances are they were frozen with sugar added. If this is the case, reduce or eliminate the sugar in this recipe.

12 ripe peaches

1¾ cups sugar or sugar substitute (I use Splenda or stevia) plus 1 tablespoon to sprinkle on top

½ cup flour, plus extra for rolling dough

2 tablespoons amaretto

1 teaspoon vanilla extract

½ teaspoon ground cinnamon

½ teaspoon iodized salt

Pie dough doubled from Pie Crust (page 114)

¼ cup all-purpose flour, for dusting work surface

Half of beaten egg saved from Pie Crust (page 114)

1. Drop peaches in boiling water (dip several at a time, depending on size of pot) for 1 to 3 minutes to loosen skins.

2. Using a slotted spoon, transfer peaches to a plate or cookie sheet and, when cool enough to handle, slip skins off.

3. Slice peaches into quarters and remove pit.

4. Slice quarters in half lengthwise then cut those slices into ¼-inch-thick pieces; put them into a large bowl. You should have 10 cups of peaches.

5. Preheat oven to 450 degrees F.

6. Mix all ingredients (except beaten egg and pie dough) with peaches in bowl and set aside.

7. If dough has been in the refrigerator, remove it from refrigerator and allow to warm to room temperature. Unwrap and divide into two portions: ⅔ (bottom crust) and ⅓ (top crust).

8. Dust clean countertop, pastry board, plastic wrap, or cloth with flour; place larger ball on dusted surface and flatten it into a rough square.

9. Roll out dough with a flour-dusted rolling pin, keeping both sides of the dough dusted with flour by turning the flattened dough over with a spatula. If edges split, repair. Roll from the center out until dough is about 14 inches long, 9 inches wide, and ⅛-inch thick.

10. Carefully roll up dough onto rolling pin and position it over a 7 x 11-inch glass pan. Unroll dough into pie pan and, using a ½ cup measuring cup, smooth out dough to conform to pan. Patch any holes or splits. Remove any excess dough around edge and add to remaining dough ball.

11. Fill pan with peach mixture and pat down top.

12. Roll out top crust, following step 9 above (except dough will be about 8 x 12 inches, and ⅛-inch thick).

13. Place rolled out top dough on top of peach mixture using rolling pin, as in step 10 and seal top crust to bottom crust at edges.

14. Using a pastry brush, brush top crust with beaten egg. Cut 8 to 10 small slits in top crust with a small knife to allow steam to escape when baking.

15. Sprinkle top crust with 1 tablespoon sugar.

16. Bake in 450 degree oven for 10 minutes. Reduce temperature to 375 degrees and bake for 40 minutes or until top crust is browned and filling bubbly.

17. Allow to partially cool before serving.

Strawberry Shortcake

Serves 10. Prep time: 1 hour.

Bake the cake the day before serving and allow it to cool. This dessert is always a spring and summer treat when strawberries are readily available.

1 box pound cake mix (about 16 ounces)

Milk/water/butter/eggs as required by the pound cake mix

2 pounds fresh strawberries

Whipped cream, for topping

1. Make pound cake batter according to directions on package.

2. Pour batter into a Bundt cake pan that has been coated with nonstick spray and then dusted with flour. (Shake off any excess flour.)

3. Bake in a preheated oven, per instructions on package.

4. When baked, cool for 10 minutes, then remove cake from Bundt pan and place on a rack to complete cooling. Set aside until serving.

5. Wash berries, remove stems, and slice.

6. To serve, cut 10 slices of pound cake and place on individual serving plates.

7. Place sliced strawberries evenly on each piece of pound cake. Top with a generous portion of whipped cream.

Ice Box Cake

Serves 12. Prep time: 30 minutes, plus refrigeration time.

This recipe is from my mother, Ruth Owen, who got it from a relative, Myrtle Windle, in the early 1940s. It was one of my favorite desserts as a kid. It is made in a large 11 x 15-inch pan, but can also be made in individual 6-ounce custard dishes.

1 (1 pound) bag white marshmallows

1 cup 2 percent milk

1 small (8 ounce) can crushed pineapple

2 cups heavy cream, whipped

20 graham crackers (2 x 4 inches) or 1 (12 ounce) box of vanilla wafers, crushed

Chocolate syrup, maraschino cherries, and/or mint sprigs, for garnish

1. In a medium saucepot over medium heat, melt marshmallows in warm milk, stirring to prevent scorching. Do not allow to boil. Cool until mixture thickens.

2. Drain pineapple, discarding juice. Fold in drained pineapple to cooled marshmallow mixture and then fold in whipped cream.

3. Line bottom of a large baking pan (about 11 x 15 inches) with half of the crushed graham crackers or vanilla wafers.

4. Carefully pour marshmallow mixture into baking pan and level with a spatula.

5. Sprinkle remaining ½ of crushed graham crackers or vanilla wafers on top of marshmallow mixture.

6. Refrigerate until mixture is firm, 1 to 2 hours.

7. Cut into squares and serve. Serving options include adding a chocolate syrup drizzle, a maraschino cherry, and/or a sprig of mint.

Mayonnaise Cake with Chocolate Icing

Serves 12. Prep time: 1 hour

This is my mother, Ruth Owen's, cake recipe with my sister, JoAnn Lohr's, icing recipe. As a kid, I always asked my mother to make this for dessert. You can add chopped nuts (walnuts, hazelnuts, or pecans) if you like to icing.

Variation: Instead of letting the cake cool and icing the cake, remove the cake from the oven, cut into serving squares using a serving spatula, top with a cube of butter, and serve.

Cake:

1 cup mayonnaise

1 cup sugar

1 cup cold water

2 cups all-purpose flour

¼ cup unsweetened cocoa powder

2 teaspoons baking soda

1 teaspoon vanilla extract

1. Preheat oven to 350 degrees F.
2. Mix first three ingredients together on a large mixing bowl until well combined.
3. Add remaining items and mix until smooth.
4. Pour batter into greased 10 x 15 x 2-inch-deep metal baking pan.
5. Bake for 30 minutes or until a toothpick inserted in center comes out clean.
6. Let cool completely before icing.

Icing:

1 cup sugar

¼ cup butter, softened

¼ cup unsweetened cocoa powder

¼ cup 2 percent milk

⅛ teaspoon iodized salt

1 teaspoon vanilla extract

1. Place all ingredients except vanilla in a medium saucepan or pot. Mix together and bring to a boil over medium heat, stirring continuously.

2. When mixture reaches a rolling boil, time for 1 minute then remove from heat.

3. Allow to cool to lukewarm then add vanilla and beat by hand to a spreading consistency.

4. Spread immediately onto cooled sheet cake, and serve by cutting squares of cake with a serving spatula.

Oatmeal Cookies

Makes 32 cookies. Prep time: 20 minutes plus baking time of 30 minutes.

With a standard-sized cookie sheet, you can bake these cookies 16 at a time. These are always good to keep on hand for an after-school snack.

8 ounces (2 sticks) salted butter, softened

½ cup sugar or sugar substitute (I use Splenda or stevia)

½ cup firmly packed dark brown sugar

2 large eggs

1 cup 2 percent milk

1 teaspoon baking soda

½ teaspoon iodized salt

1 teaspoon ground cinnamon

1 teaspoon vanilla extract

1¾ cups all-purpose flour

3 cups thick-rolled, old-fashioned oats

½ cup chopped walnuts

1 cup chocolate or butterscotch chips

½ cup raisins

1. Preheat oven to 375 degrees F.

2. Using an electric mixer, cream first 9 ingredients until smooth and fluffy.

3. Add flour and mix well, scraping down bowl as needed.

4. Add oats and continue mixing.

5. Add walnuts, chips, and raisins; mix on slow speed until combined.

6. Coat cookie sheet with olive oil and form half of cookie dough into 16 1½-inch balls and drop individually on cookie sheet.

7. Bake for 10 to 12 minutes or until cookies are browned.

8. Remove cookies from cookie sheet using a metal spatula; place on paper towels to cool.

9. Repeat with second half of cookie dough.

10. When cool (assuming they aren't all eaten) transfer to plastic bags and refrigerate or freeze.

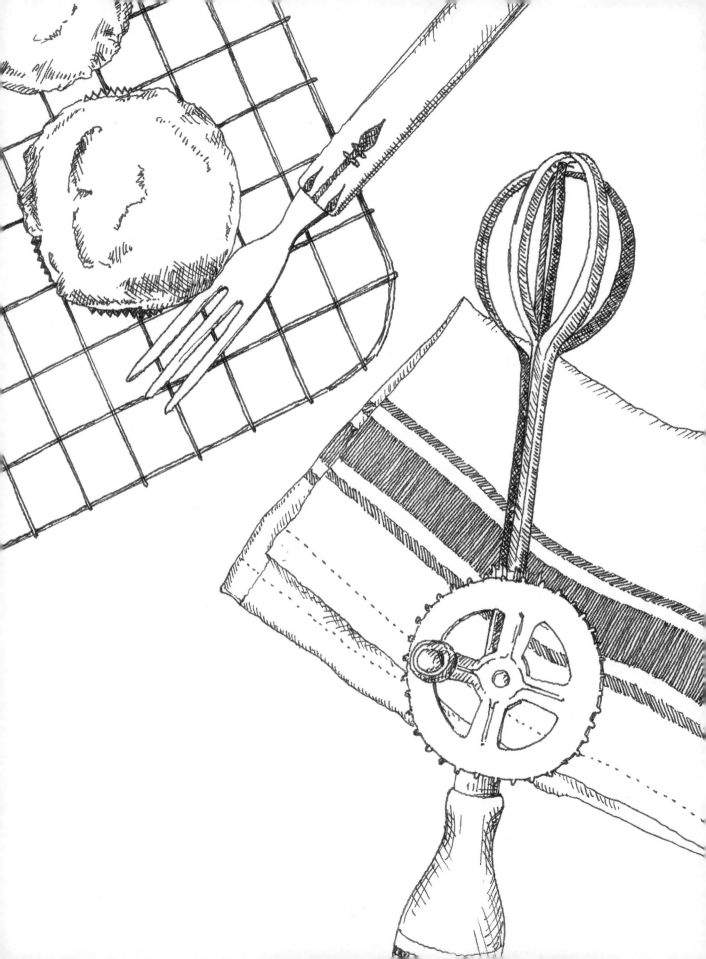

Breakfast Dishes

No matter how busy it can get in the morning, it's important to start the day with a good breakfast. Fixing eggs, pancakes, or hot cereal does not take long—and when served with fruit and milk, these dishes provide a real nutritional boost. Cold breakfast cereals served with milk and fruit can also be used once in a while if time is really short, but avoid those that are loaded with sugar. Keep in mind that most cold cereals are very expensive when compared with hot cereal.

I have not included how to cook eggs, toast, bacon, ham, and sausage, which I assume you know how to do. I have included only one hot cereal recipe, assuming that you know how to prepare hot cereal by following the instructions on the box or the instructions provided with bulk purchases. Hot cereals are economical, nutritious, and easy to make. What I have included are a few special items that I fix for breakfast—most for everyday consumption and some for weekend mornings or a special brunch.

Breakfast Muffins

Makes 1 dozen muffins. Prep time: 25 minutes, plus 35 minutes baking time.

If you are tired of purchased muffins, try these—they are delicious. Make a batch for Sunday breakfast and freeze half for breakfast on the following Wednesday or Thursday. Just warm them (gently) in the microwave and breakfast is ready. Note: If you do not have muffin tins or paper muffin cups, spray nonstick olive oil in an 8 x 8-inch glass baking pan and pour the batter right into the pan. To serve, let cool for 5 minutes and cut into pieces.

1 cup whole wheat flour

1 cup all-purpose flour

¼ cup ground flax seed

½ cup steel-cut oatmeal

¼ cup wheat bran

⅓ cup olive oil

8 tablespoons (1 stick) butter, melted

⅔ cup sugar or sugar substitute (I use Splenda or stevia)

2 large eggs, beaten

1½ cups 2 percent milk

2 teaspoons baking powder

½ teaspoon iodized salt

1 teaspoon ground cinnamon

½ teaspoon ground mace

½ cup raisins

½ cup walnut pieces

½ apple, peeled, cored, and cut into ¼-inch diced pieces

1. Preheat oven to 400 degrees F.

2. Spray or rub olive oil into cups of a standard 12-muffin pan or fill with paper cupcake liners.

3. Mix all ingredients together in a bowl.

4. Divide batter between muffin cups, filling them about two-thirds full.

5. Bake for about 30 minutes or until a toothpick inserted into center comes out clean.

6. Let cool for 5 minutes before serving.

Cinnamon Rolls

Makes 18 rolls. Prep time: about 2 hours and 20 minutes.

Up through step 9 can be done ahead of time and frozen or refrigerated. Thaw thoroughly before proceeding to step 10. This recipe uses a cake mix and is from my sister, JoAnn Lohr. These are delicious. Bring a batch to the office and watch them disappear!

Dough:

1 (15.25 ounce) box vanilla cake mix. I use Betty Crocker. (Use dry contents only; do not assemble batter.)

4 cups all-purpose flour

2 (0.25 ounce) packets active dry yeast (5 teaspoons)

1 teaspoon iodized salt

2 cups water, 120 to 130 degrees F

Filling:

2 tablespoons butter, softened

½ cup sugar

1 tablespoon ground cinnamon

1 cup raisins

¾ cup chopped walnuts

Icing:

2 tablespoons butter, softened

1 cup powdered sugar

1 teaspoon vanilla extract

1. Dissolve yeast in warm water. Let set until bubbly, about 10 minutes. Add salt and stir to dissolve.

2. Using a stand mixer with the large bowl and dough hook, add yeast mixture and dry cake mix; mix well.

3. With mixer on low/medium speed, gradually add flour to mixture until it becomes a very soft dough. (You may not need all 4 cups of flour.)

4. Cover bowl with plastic and let rise in a warm place for 1 hour or until doubled.

5. Turn out dough onto a lightly floured surface and pat (do not knead) into a 12 x 12-inch square that is ½-inch thick.

6. Spread filling ingredients evenly onto dough, keeping ½ inch away from edges.

7. Roll dough into a cylinder, Seal ends and edges by squeezing dough together.

8. Using a serrated knife, cut dough at right angles to the roll into 18 pieces.

9. Place rolls (cut sides up) into an 11 x 14-inch ovenproof dish, coated with shortening.

10. Preheat oven to 350 degrees F.

11. Place dish in a warm place and cover with a towel. Let rise 15 minutes.

12. Bake for 15 to 20 minutes. Check to make sure innermost rolls are fully baked. If they are still doughy, bake for another 5 to 10 minutes.

13. Remove from oven and cool for 10 minutes.

14. In a small bowl, prepare icing by mixing all ingredients into spreading consistency.

15. Spread icing over rolls and serve.

Old Goat's Breakfast Cereal

Serves 2. Prep time: 12 minutes.

This cereal provides 17 grams of fiber per serving, which is more than half of the 30 grams of fiber recommended for men per day. If you buy oats, bran, flax seed, and walnuts in bulk, this breakfast costs less than 50 cents per serving.

2 cups water

½ cup steel-cut or thick rolled oats

½ cup wheat bran

¼ cup ground flax seed

½ cup chopped walnuts

1 teaspoon ground cinnamon

½ teaspoon iodized salt

1 cup fat-free half-and-half or 2 percent milk

2 tablespoons sugar, brown sugar, or sugar substitute

1. In a small saucepan over high heat, bring water, salt, cinnamon, walnuts, oats, and bran to a boil.

2. Reduce heat to medium low and cook for 10 minutes, stirring occasionally.

3. Turn off heat, add ground flax seeds and mix thoroughly. Let sit for 1 minute.

4. Serve with fat-free half-and-half or milk, and brown sugar, sugar, or sugar substitute.

Biscuits and Sausage Gravy

Serves 6. Prep time: 20 minutes. You will need a 9- to 10-inch round baking pan for biscuits. This is a good side dish for scrambled eggs. Biscuits with gravy has been a traditional dish in my family for as long as I can remember. This dish was not made very often but when it was made, it was appreciated. You can also make this dish for dinner and serve with steamed green beans or asparagus.

Biscuits:

2 cups all-purpose flour

2 teaspoons baking powder

½ teaspoon iodized salt

½ cup vegetable shortening that has been chilled in refrigerator

¾ cup buttermilk

1 teaspoon bacon grease or shortening, to grease baking pan

Gravy:

½ pound (1 cup) breakfast sausage

½ cup all-purpose flour

3 cups warm 2 percent milk (heat to 100 degrees F in microwave)

1 teaspoon iodized salt

1 teaspoon freshly ground white pepper

1. Preheat oven to 425 degrees F.

2. Break up and brown sausage in a medium-sized skillet over medium heat, setting aside when done.

3. While sausage is cooking, begin making biscuits: mix flour, baking powder, and salt together in a mixing bowl.

4. Using a pastry cutter or fork, add shortening to bowl and cut in to evenly distribute.

5. Add buttermilk and, using a wooden spoon, quickly mix to distribute liquid. Place dough on a floured surface and pat into a 10-inch circle about ½-inch thick.

6. Grease biscuit baking pan.

7. Cut dough into 2½-inch rounds using a biscuit/cookie cutter or tin can. Arrange them in baking dish. You should have about 12 biscuits in the pan.

8. Bake biscuits for about 12 minutes, until they are golden brown.

9. While biscuits are baking, put pan with sausage back onto medium heat. Add ½ cup flour to cooked sausage and stir until mixed.

10. Slowly pour warm milk into flour/sausage mixture, stirring thoroughly until gravy bubbles and thickens.

11. Stir in salt and pepper. Keep warm.

12. When biscuits are done, remove from oven and take them out of baking pan.

13. To serve, place 2 biscuits on each plate and cover with gravy.

Eggs Benedict

Serves 4. Prep time: about 30 minutes.

This recipe uses only cooked eggs. Raw (runny) egg yolks are a growth medium for bacteria, including salmonella. Thus the hollandaise sauce and poached eggs in this recipe are cooked to 160 degrees F in order to kill any bacteria that may be in the eggs.

Hollandaise sauce:

4 large egg yolks

1 tablespoon fresh lemon juice

¼ teaspoon Worcestershire sauce

¼ teaspoon freshly ground white pepper

¼ teaspoon iodized salt

1 cup butter (2 sticks), melted

Muffins and Canadian bacon:

4 English muffins, split in half

8 slices Canadian bacon

Butter, for spreading on muffin halves

Dash of paprika, for garnish

Parsley sprigs, for garnish

Poached eggs:

8 large eggs

1 teaspoon white vinegar

Hollandaise sauce:

1. Pour about 2 cups of water into bottom of a double boiler and turn heat to medium.

2. Insert top pan and check to verify that the water is not touching top pan.

3. Allow water to come to a gentle simmer and reduce heat to low.

4. In top of double boiler, add yolks, lemon juice, and Worcestershire sauce. Whisk continuously until mixture coats a metal spoon, bubbles at edges, or reaches 160 degrees. Remove from heat.

5. Slowly whisk in butter, one tablespoon at a time.

6. Continue adding butter until it is all incorporated into sauce.

7. Add salt and pepper and stir.

8. Remove from heat, cover, and keep warm.

Prepare remaining items:

1. Preheat broiler for toasting muffins.

2. Add 3 inches of water to a large sauce pan and, over medium heat, bring water to a gentle simmer.

3. While water is heating, place muffins on a cookie sheet cut sides up; toast under broiler until brown.

4. Butter muffins and set aside, keeping warm.

5. In a skillet over medium to high heat, brown Canadian bacon on both sides; remove and keep warm.

6. When poaching water is simmering, add vinegar to water.

7. Break eggs into simmering water, being careful not to break yolks.

8. Cook eggs for 5 to 6 minutes or until yolks are cooked.

9. Remove eggs with a slotted spoon and place on a warm plate.

Assemble:

1. On each serving plate, place 2 halves of English muffins side by side with toasted sides up.

2. Place a slice of Canadian bacon on each muffin half.

3. Place a poached egg on each muffin half.

4. Pour hollandaise sauce over each assembly.

5. Garnish tops with a dash of paprika and a sprig of parsley.

6. Serve at once.

Bacon Quiche

Serves 16. Prep time: about 1 hour if pie crusts are already made.

This recipe makes two 9½-inch-round quiches. Serve one and freeze one for later use. To freeze, cover the quiche with plastic wrap. To use, remove the quiche from the freezer and allow it to return to room temperature before baking. If you are serving for breakfast, take it out of the freezer the night before. Remove the plastic wrap and heat in a 350-degree F oven for 10 minutes or until the center is warm. It can also be heated in the microwave but cover the top with a paper towel.

Pie Crust (page 114)

1 pound thick-sliced bacon, cut into 1-inch-long pieces

8 large eggs, lightly beaten

½ cup diced yellow onion

2 cups 2 percent milk

3 cups (¾ pound) shredded Swiss cheese

1 (6½ ounce) can mushrooms, stems and pieces

⅛ teaspoon ground nutmeg

½ teaspoon iodized salt

1 teaspoon freshly ground white pepper

1. Preheat oven to 400 degrees F.

2. Dust clean countertop, pastry board, or pastry cloth with flour; place pie dough on dusted surface, cut in half, and flatten both halves into disks.

3. Roll out each half with a flour-dusted rolling pin, keeping both sides of dough dusted with flour by turning flattened dough over with a spatula. If edges split, repair. Roll dough from the center outward until it is about 12 inches in diameter and ⅛-inch thick.

4. Carefully roll dough onto rolling pin and position it over your 9½-inch pie pan. Unroll dough into pie pan and, using a ½-cup measuring cup, smooth out dough to conform to pan. Patch any holes or splits. Remove excess dough around the edge.

5. Repeat steps 2 through 4 for second quiche.

6. Chill crusts in refrigerator for 15 minutes then bake in preheated oven for 10 to 15 minutes or until they are slightly brown.

7. Remove from oven and set aside to cool.

8. Lower oven temperature to 350 degrees.

9. In a skillet, cook bacon until crisp over medium heat.

10. Remove bacon from skillet, drain and set aside.

11. Dispose of bacon grease, keeping 2 tablespoons in skillet.

12. Return skillet to stove; add onions and cook, stirring, until they are translucent.

13. Add mushrooms and cook for 1 minute.

14. Transfer skillet contents to a medium-sized bowl and add eggs, bacon, milk, cheese, nutmeg, salt, and pepper. Stir to mix.

15. Pour egg mixture equally into each shell.

16. Place quiches in oven.

17. Bake for about 40 minutes, until center is cooked.

18. Remove from oven and let cool for 5 minutes before serving.

Eggs Farley

Serves 8 to 10. Prep time: about 30 minutes to boil and peel eggs, 30 minutes for sautéing onions and making white sauce, and 50 minutes baking time.

The eggs for this recipe should be boiled and peeled a day or two before. Do the rest (except baking) the evening before, cover and refrigerate. Leftovers can be refrigerated and warmed in the microwave in a covered pan. This is a great brunch egg dish. When the kids were growing up, they would ask to have this dish the morning after their sleepover birthday parties.

2 dozen large eggs

6 large yellow onions, peeled and sliced into rings about ¼-inch thick (I know this looks like too many, but it is correct!)

8 tablespoons (1 stick) salted butter

½ cup all-purpose flour

3 cups half-and-half

1 tablespoon Dijon mustard

2 teaspoons iodized salt

2 teaspoons freshly ground white pepper

6 saltine crackers (2 inches square), crushed

1 teaspoon paprika, for garnish

1. In a large pot, cover eggs with water and a lid and bring to a boil. Turn off heat and let eggs cook on burner in hot water for 12 minutes. Pour off hot water and add cold water and ice to cool eggs thoroughly.

2. When eggs are cold, peel them under water, dry, and set aside in refrigerator.

3. In a large skillet over medium heat, melt butter and add onions. Cover.

4. Remove cover and stir onions. Replace cover. Continue removing cover and stirring until all onions are cooked but not brown (about 15 minutes).

5. Using a colander and a bowl to catch the liquid, drain onions and set aside to cool.

6. Return liquid drained from onions to skillet, and over medium heat, add flour. Whisk until flour is well mixed with liquid.

7. Add half-and-half and whisk continuously until mixture begins to boil.

8. Add mustard, salt, and pepper; continue whisking for 5 minutes. Remove sauce from heat and set aside.

9. Preheat oven to 325 degrees F.

10. In a 9 x 13-inch baking dish, assemble dish:

First layer: 6 eggs, diced and chopped into small crumbles

Second layer: One-third of the onions, spread evenly

Third layer: 6 eggs, diced and chopped

Fourth layer: One-third of the onions, spread evenly

Fifth layer: 6 eggs, diced and chopped

Sixth layer: Last one-third of onions, spread evenly

Last layer: Last 6 eggs, diced and chopped

11. Top with crackers and a dash of paprika.

12. Bake, covered with a lid or aluminum foil, for 30 minutes.

13. Remove cover and continue to bake for 15 minutes or until dish is browned and bubbly.

14. Remove from oven and let cool for 5 minutes before serving.

Whole Wheat Buttermilk Pancakes

Makes six 6-inch pancakes. Prep time: 10 minutes, plus cooking time.

These are very nutritious pancakes that will start your day off right. If you have fresh blueberries or strawberries, add them to top of a stack of these pancakes for a real treat.

½ cup whole wheat flour

½ cup all-purpose flour

¼ cup ground flax seed

¼ cup wheat bran

2 teaspoons baking powder

½ teaspoon iodized salt

¼ teaspoon ground cinnamon

½ teaspoon vanilla extract

1 large egg, beaten

2 tablespoons olive oil, plus more for greasing skillet or griddle

2 cups buttermilk

1. Preheat skillet or griddle over medium heat.
2. Mix all ingredients together in a bowl.
3. Grease skillet or griddle with oil.
4. Pour batter into skillet or griddle to form 6-inch pancakes.
5. Turn each pancake over when bottom is golden brown.
6. Remove pancake when fully cooked through and golden brown on both sides.
7. Serve with butter or margarine, maple syrup, jam, or jelly.

Whole Wheat Buttermilk Waffles

Makes six to seven 6-inch waffles. Prep time: 10 minutes plus cooking time.

I often serve these for dinner with fresh sliced strawberries and whipped cream topping.

½ cup whole wheat flour

½ cup all-purpose flour

¼ cup ground flax seed

¼ cup wheat bran

2 teaspoons baking powder

½ teaspoon iodized salt

½ teaspoon vanilla extract

¼ teaspoon ground cinnamon

2 large eggs, beaten

¼ cup olive oil

1¾ cup buttermilk

1. Preheat waffle iron.

2. Mix all ingredients together in a bowl.

3. Pour batter into preheated waffle iron to fill waffle grid and close lid.

4. Remove waffle from waffle iron when "done" light comes on or when waffle is a deep golden brown.

5. Repeat steps 3 and 4 until all waffles are cooked.

6. Serve with butter or margarine, maple syrup, jam, or jelly.

French Toast

Makes 4 pieces. Prep time: 10 minutes.

French toast is easy to make for breakfast. I would serve it once a week since it was so popular.

4 slices homemade bread or purchased French bread

3 large eggs, beaten

½ cup fat-free half-and-half or 2 percent milk

½ teaspoon iodized salt

½ teaspoon ground cinnamon

½ teaspoon vanilla extract

Olive oil, for frying

1. Preheat skillet or griddle over medium heat.

2. Mix eggs, half-and-half, salt, cinnamon, and vanilla in a pie pan or other flat dish with sides large enough for bread slice.

3. Grease skillet or griddle with oil.

4. Dip a slice of bread into egg mixture briefly and then turn over briefly. (If you leave bread in egg mixture too long, it will fall apart.)

5. Place bread into skillet and cook for 2 to 3 minutes or until golden brown.

6. Turn bread slice over and cook for another 2 to 3 minutes, until golden brown.

7. Transfer French toast to a plate, keep warm, and repeat steps 4 through 7 until all bread pieces are cooked.

8. Serve with butter or margarine, maple syrup, jam, or jelly.

Breads

Breads are fun to make even though they take time. Nothing is better than warm home-made bread. You need very little in the way of special cooking equipment, but having a modern stand mixer with a bread hook certainly makes mixing and kneading faster and easier. For baking bread, there are three options: In the oven in ovenproof glass or metal loaf baking pans; in the oven on a flat surface such as a cookie sheet or pizza stone; or outside in a wood-fired oven.

If you use the outdoor wood-fired oven, the bread can be baked in a cast-iron Dutch oven (without the lid) or baked directly on the hearth of the oven. The fire should be started about one hour before the bread goes in the oven so that the hearth has time to reach 400 degrees F. (The temperature can be checked using an inexpensive infrared heat gun.) Before placing the bread in the oven, brush the fire to the back and sides of the hearth and wet mop the center of the hearth where the bread will go. This removes any ash from the hearth that may stick to the bread. Rotate the bread four times during the baking period to brown the top crust evenly. Keep the hearth temperature between 375 and 400 degrees as the bread bakes. The baking time will be close to the times listed in recipes. When the bread is done, use oven mitts to remove the bread from the oven.

Making your own bread is very cost effective, assuming you buy the flours and grains in bulk, but don't buy more than you will use in a short period of time. (If you have more than you can keep, package it tightly and store in the freezer.)

In this chapter, you'll find recipes for breads that use predominantly all-purpose white flour, and others that have a higher percentage of whole wheat or rye flours. Feel free to add other variety grains, and try varying the toppings from cornmeal to sesame seeds to poppy seeds. Also included are some specialty breads and a dinner roll recipe that I'd love for you to try—it has been a favorite in my family for forty years.

Cornbread

Serves 16. Prep time: 30 minutes, plus 30 minutes to bake.

2 cups yellow cornmeal

2 cups all-purpose flour

⅔ cup pure olive oil

¼ cup sugar

2 large eggs, beaten

2 cups 2 percent milk

2 tablespoons baking powder

2 teaspoons iodized salt

1. Preheat oven to 400 degrees F.

2. Mix ingredients together in a bowl.

3. Coat sides and bottom of an 11 x 15-inch ovenproof glass pan with olive oil.

4. Pour batter into pan; level top.

5. Bake for 25 minutes or until top is brown and a toothpick comes out clean when inserted into center of dish.

6. To serve, let cool briefly then cut into 16 pieces. Cornbread is always best the day it is baked. If you have extra, wrap it well and freeze (up to 2 months) for another time.

Skillet Cornbread with Bacon

Serves 8. Prep time: 35 minutes, plus 30 minutes to bake.

This is a good side dish with beans or soup. Serve with butter or margarine and honey. I make this in a No. 8 cast-iron skillet (about 10½ inches in diameter), and it comes out crisp and beautifully browned. I use a cast-iron skillet because I can fry the bacon in it and then use the same pan (without cleaning it) to bake the cornbread. I'm sure you have seen cooks dirty lots of dishes in the process of cooking a meal . . . not me! In case you haven't noticed in reading this book, I use cast iron a lot because it lasts forever, is inexpensive to buy new or used, and can be used on a grill, in a campfire, in the oven, or on the stove top . . . how versatile is that?

2 strips of bacon

1 cup yellow cornmeal

1 cup all-purpose flour

1 tablespoon sugar

1 teaspoon iodized salt

1 tablespoon baking powder

1 large egg, beaten

⅓ cup pure olive oil

1 cup buttermilk or 2 percent milk

1. Fry bacon in skillet until brown. Remove bacon from skillet, leaving 1 tablespoon of grease.

2. Chop bacon into small pieces and save to add to batter. Dispose of remaining grease. Make sure bottom and sides of skillet are well greased.

3. Preheat oven to 400 degrees F.

4. Mix remaining ingredients, including bacon bits, in a bowl.

5. Pour batter into skillet and level top.

6. Bake for 25 minutes. The top should be golden brown.

7. Remove skillet from oven with oven mitt and allow to cool for 5 minutes on a stove burner.

8. Place a clean towel on your countertop and carefully invert hot pan onto it; cornbread should drop out.

9. Cut into serving pieces and serve.

Irish Soda Bread

Makes 1 round loaf. Prep time: 10 minutes, plus 45 minutes to bake.

You can bake Irish Soda Bread in an outdoor wood-fired oven with a baking surface temperature of 400 degrees F (start the fire 1 hour before starting this recipe) or in a kitchen oven as described below. Use a large mixer with a dough hook to mix and knead the dough, or mix by hand. This recipe does not use yeast and requires no rising time. I serve this with Corned Beef and Cabbage (page 66).

3¼ cups all-purpose flour, plus extra for kneading

1 teaspoon sugar

1 teaspoon sea salt

1 teaspoon baking soda

1½ to 2 cups buttermilk

1. Preheat oven to 375 degrees F.

2. In the bowl of an electric stand mixer with the dough hook or in a large mixing bowl, combine flour, sugar, salt, and soda with one cup buttermilk and mix thoroughly.

3. Slowly pour in remaining ½ to 1 cup of buttermilk, adding only enough to make dough soft but not sticky.

4. Turn bread dough onto a floured work surface and form into a round loaf about 1½ inch at thickest point.

5. Cut a deep cross in top and down sides.

6. Place loaf on a greased baking sheet or pizza stone and place in preheated oven.

7. Bake for 45 minutes or until loaf sounds hollow when tapped on bottom.

8. Remove loaf from oven and allow to cool briefly before serving.

Oatmeal Bread

Makes one 10-inch-round loaf or 2 loaf-pan loaves. Prep time: 30 minutes, plus 1½ hours to rise and 40 minutes to bake.

Use a large mixer with a dough hook to mix and knead the dough or do it by hand mixing and kneading. This bread is so good fresh out of the oven and served with soups. It will be eaten before you know it.

2 (0.25) ounce packets active dry yeast (5 teaspoons)

3 cups water at 105 degrees F. (Heat water in a jar or glass bowl in microwave. Check temperature with a thermometer; 105 degrees is just slightly warm.)

6 cups all-purpose flour, plus extra for kneading

1 cup thick-cut rolled oats

¼ cup ground flax seed

½ cup wheat bran

1 tablespoon sea salt

½ cup yellow cornmeal, for dusting loaf

1. In the bowl of an electric stand mixer with the dough hook or in a large mixing bowl, dissolve yeast in warm water.

2. Add 1 cup of flour, rolled oats, ground flax seed, bran, and salt; mix thoroughly.

3. Add another cup of flour and continue to mix.

4. Add remaining flour a cup at a time and continue mixing, stopping when dough is stiff and elastic. You may not need all the flour.

5. Cover dough with a cloth and set in a warm place to rise for 1 hour.

6. After 1 hour, remove dough from mixing bowl and place on a well-floured bread-board or countertop.

7. Knead dough, adding flour as necessary, until dough is no longer sticky (about 5 minutes). Form into a ball or into 2 loaves if using loaf pans.

8. Remove excess flour from board and scatter cornmeal.

9. Roll each loaf in cornmeal to coat dough.

10. Place loaves in greased loaf pans, a Dutch oven, or onto a pizza stone. Cover with clean cloth and allow to rise for about 30 minutes in a warm location. Loaves should nearly double in size.

11. Preheat oven to 375 degrees F.

12. Bake for 40 minutes or until bread is lightly browned on top and loaf sounds hollow when tapped.

13. Using oven mitts, remove bread from oven and pans.

14. Allow to cool on a cooling rack before slicing.

15. Refrigerate bread and use within one week, or freeze for later use.

Whole Wheat Bread

Makes one 10-inch-round loaf or 2 loaf-pan loaves. Prep time: 30 minutes, plus 1½ hours to rise and 40 minutes to bake.

Use a large mixer with a dough hook to mix and knead the dough or do it by hand mixing and kneading. This bread is very hardy and crunchy due to the wheat berries. Try it fresh out of the oven with butter for a special treat.

¼ cup hard red winter wheat berries

½ cup steel-cut oatmeal

2 (0.25 ounce) packets active dry yeast (5 teaspoons)

3 cups water at 105 degrees F. (Heat water in a jar or glass bowl in microwave. Check temperature with a thermometer; 105 degrees is just slightly warm.)

4½ cups all-purpose flour, plus extra for kneading

2 cups whole wheat flour

¼ cup dark molasses

4 teaspoons sea salt

¼ cup yellow cornmeal, for dusting loaf

1. Boil wheat berries in 2 cups water for 20 minutes. Add oatmeal and cook another 10 minutes. Drain excess water through a strainer; set aside to cool.
2. After starting step 1, dissolve yeast in warm water in mixing bowl.
3. Add 1 cup of the all-purpose flour and all of the whole wheat flour, molasses, and salt; mix thoroughly.
4. Add another cup of flour and continue to mix.
5. Add cooked wheat berries and oatmeal.
6. Add remaining flour 1 cup at a time and continue mixing.
7. Cover dough with a cloth and set in a warm place to rise for 1 hour.
8. After 1 hour of rising, remove dough from mixing bowl and place on a well-floured breadboard or countertop.

9. Knead dough, adding flour as necessary, until dough is no longer sticky. Form into a round ball or into 2 loaves if using loaf pans.

10. Remove excess flour from board and scatter cornmeal.

11. Roll each loaf in cornmeal to coat dough.

12. Preheat oven to 375 degrees F.

13. Place loaves into greased loaf pans, into a Dutch oven, or onto a pizza stone. Cover with clean cloth and allow to rise for 30 minutes in a warm location, until nearly double in size.

14. Bake for 40 minutes or until bread is lightly browned on top and loaf sounds hollow when tapped.

15. Using oven mitts, remove bread from oven then gently release bread from baking pans or Dutch oven.

16. Allow to cool on a cooling rack before slicing.

17. Refrigerate bread and use within one week, or freeze for later use.

Quick Dinner Rolls

Makes 2 dozen rolls. Prep time: 30 minutes, plus 5 minutes to rise and 15 minutes to bake.

Because it is faster, it is better to use a large mixer with a dough hook to mix and knead this dough than hand mixing and kneading. You will need one or two large cookie sheets for baking these rolls. They are easy to make in less than 1 hour and are always a welcome addition to your special dinners.

1¾ cups 2 percent milk

2 (0.25 ounce) packets active dry yeast (5 teaspoons)

½ cup water at 105 degrees F. (Heat water in a jar or glass bowl in microwave. Check temperature with a thermometer; 105 degrees is just slightly warm.)

½ cup (1 stick) melted butter, divided

1 tablespoon sugar

1 large egg, well-beaten

2 teaspoons sea salt

6 cups all-purpose flour, plus extra for dusting

1. Preheat oven to 400 degrees F.

2. Scald milk in glass container in microwave. (Scalding is heating to just below boiling, when a skin forms on top of milk.)

3. Let milk cool to about 110 degrees. (Set in ice water to speed this up.)

4. In mixing bowl of a large stand mixer, dissolve yeast in warm water.

5. Add cooled scalded milk, melted butter, sugar, egg, and salt; mix on low speed, using dough hook.

6. Add 2 cups of flour and mix very thoroughly. Scrape down sides of bowl.

7. Add rest of flour 1 cup at a time and continue to mix until dough can be handled. It may still be slightly sticky.

8. Scrape dough from mixing bowl and place on a well-floured breadboard or countertop.

9. Roll out dough to about ½-inch thick.

10. Cut 2½-inch-diameter rounds, using a cookie or biscuit cutter or tin can.

11. Dip one side of the rounds in remaining melted butter and fold in half, with buttered side on inside.

12. Place on a greased cookie sheet.

13. Repeat steps 10 through 12 until all dough is used (reroll scraps as needed). You should have about 24 rolls.

14. Allow rolls to rise in a warm location for 5 minutes.

15. Bake for 15 minutes or until rolls are light brown on top.

16. Remove from oven and serve warm.

17. Refrigerate unused rolls and use within one week, or freeze, well wrapped, for later use.

Rye Dinner Rolls

Makes 18 rolls. Prep time: 30 minutes, plus 1½ hours to rise, and 25 minutes to bake.

You will need a large cookie sheet (12 x 17-inch) to bake these on. As an alternative to round rolls, shape the dough into small oblong loaves, bake and cool, and then slice in half lengthwise and use to make Reuben sandwiches. Delicious!

1 (0.25 ounce) packet active dry yeast (2½ teaspoons)

¾ cup water at 105 degrees F. (Heat water in a jar or glass bowl in microwave. Check temperature with a thermometer; 105 degrees is just slightly warm.)

1 cup warm 2 percent milk, at 105 degrees F.

2 tablespoons butter, melted

1 tablespoon sea salt

3 cups all-purpose flour, plus extra for dusting

2 cups rye flour

1 tablespoon whole caraway seed

Vegetable oil, for greasing cookie sheet

¼ cup yellow cornmeal for dusting rolls

1. In mixing bowl, dissolve yeast in warm water. Let rest for 10 minutes.

2. Add milk, butter, and salt and start mixing.

3. Add 1 cup of flour and mix thoroughly. Scrape down sides of bowl.

4. Add another cup of flour and continue to mix.

5. Add last cup of flour and continue mixing.

6. Add 1 cup of rye flour and continue mixing.

7. Add last cup of rye flour and caraway seed; mix for 5 minutes on low speed. Dough will be dense but still sticky.

8. Cover dough with a cloth and set in a warm place to rise for 1 hour or until dough has nearly doubled in size.

9. Remove dough from mixing bowl and place on a well-floured breadboard or countertop.

10. Knead dough, adding flour if necessary, for 5 minutes, until dough is no longer sticky.

11. Place cornmeal in a small bowl.

12. Grease cookie sheet.

13. Cut pieces of dough from large ball and roll between hands until a ball is formed; it should be about 1½ inches in diameter.

14. Roll dough ball in cornmeal to coat.

15. Roll once more between hands then place on greased cookie sheet.

16. Repeat until all dough is used. (You should have 18 rolls on cookie sheet.)

17. Allow rolls to rise in a warm location for 30 minutes uncovered.

18. Preheat oven to 375 degrees F.

19. Bake for 25 minutes or until rolls are lightly browned.

20. Remove from oven and serve warm.

21. Refrigerate unused rolls and use within one week, or freeze for later use.

Yorkshire Pudding

Serves 8. Prep time: 30 minutes.

Yorkshire pudding is not a pudding—it's more like an unsweetened puffed pastry. It is a delicious side dish served with beef roasts and au jus. It can be made in a muffin tin or (my preference) in ovenproof, 6-ounce glass custard cups. Serve the "puddings" as soon as you remove them from the oven to prevent them from shrinking. I fix Yorkshire pudding to accompany my Beef Rib Roast Au Jus (page 103). Try it once and you'll be hooked.

2 cups all-purpose flour

2 cups 2 percent milk

4 large eggs

1 teaspoon iodized salt

½ cup beef drippings from beef rib roasting pan (see Beef Rib Roast Au Jus, page 103). If you don't have beef drippings, you can also use bacon grease, which would bring a different taste.

1. Preheat oven to 450 degrees F.

2. Using a wire whip or electric mixer, vigorously beat all ingredients together in a bowl. (This is critical for success.)

3. Place 1 teaspoon of beef drippings from prime rib roasting pan in each of the custard cups. With a pastry brush or paper towel, spread drippings to generously coat inside of cup completely. Leave any remaining beef drippings in cup.

4. Place cups on a small cookie sheet and place in hot oven for 5 minutes.

5. Remove cookie sheet and cups; quickly pour batter into each cup filling them about ¾ full.

6. Quickly return pan to oven and bake for 10 minutes.

7. Reduce oven temperature to 350 degrees and bake an additional 15 to 20 minutes, until they are puffy (double in size) and nicely browned.

8. Remove from oven, pop out of baking cups, and serve hot au jus.

Pumpkin Bread

Makes 1 loaf (16 slices). Prep time: 30 minutes to prepare pumpkin plus 15 minutes to assemble and 1 hour and 20 minutes to bake.

This is a good way to use up those excess Rouge Vif d' Etampes (Cinderella) pumpkins, other pie pumpkins, or winter squash from the garden. For convenience, you may also use canned pumpkin. This moist quick bread is delicious and dairy free.

2 cups cooked fresh pumpkin or 1 (16 ounce) can pumpkin puree

2 large eggs, beaten

3 cups all-purpose flour

2 teaspoons baking powder

1 teaspoon baking soda

1 teaspoon iodized salt

1 teaspoon ground cinnamon

¼ teaspoon ground allspice

½ cup brown sugar

½ cup sugar-free maple syrup

¼ cup pure olive oil

½ cup chopped walnuts

½ cup raisins

1. To cook pumpkin, cut in half, remove seeds and pulp, peel, and cut into 1-inch cubes.

2. Place cubes in a pot and add water to cover.

3. Cook over medium heat until pumpkin meat is tender (about 15 minutes).

4. Remove from heat, drain liquid, and set aside to cool briefly.

5. Mash pumpkin with a potato masher and measure out 2 cups for this recipe. Remaining pumpkin can be frozen for later use.

6. Preheat oven to 350 degrees F.

7. In a large mixing bowl, mix 2 cups of pumpkin with eggs.

8. Add remaining ingredients (except nuts and raisins) and stir with a spoon until well mixed.

9. Add nuts and raisins and mix to distribute evenly.

10. Place batter in a greased 9 x 5-inch loaf or bread pan.

11. Bake for 1 hour and 15 minutes. Top should be golden brown or until a toothpick inserted into center comes out clean.

12. Remove from oven using oven mitts and cool for 5 minutes on a wire rack or stove burner.

13. Invert pan over towel to release bread. (You may need to free edges and bottom with a knife or spatula.)

14. Let cool a few minutes to make cutting into serving pieces easier.

Zucchini Bread

Makes 2 loaves (16 slices). Prep time: 30 minutes, plus 1 hour and 35 minutes to bake.

This dairy-free recipe is a great way to use up excess summer squash (green or yellow zucchini, crookneck, or pattypan) from the garden. Use one loaf and freeze the other for use later.

2 cups grated zucchini or other summer squash

3 large eggs, beaten until frothy

3 cups all-purpose flour

1 cup sugar-free maple syrup

1 teaspoon baking powder

1 teaspoon baking soda

1 teaspoon iodized salt

2 teaspoons ground cinnamon

1 teaspoon vanilla

1 cup pure olive oil

½ cup chopped walnuts

½ cup raisins

Shortening, to grease loaf pans

1. Preheat oven to 350 degrees F.

2. In a large bowl, thoroughly mix all ingredients except for zucchini, walnuts, and raisins.

3. Fold in zucchini, walnuts, and raisins until they're evenly distributed.

4. Grease 2 ovenproof 9 x 5-inch loaf or bread pans.

5. Place an equal amount of batter in each loaf pan.

6. Bake for 1 hour and 30 minutes or until a toothpick inserted into center comes out clean. Top should be golden brown.

7. Remove from oven using oven mitts, and cool for 5 minutes on a stove burner.

8. Invert pan over towel to remove bread. (You may need to free edges and bottom with a knife or spatula if stuck.)

9. Let cool a few minutes to make cutting into serving pieces easier.

Sauces and Condiments

Knowing how to make sauces and condiments can provide flexibility and interest in preparing meals. No need to make a run to the store for shrimp cocktail sauce when you can make your own from ingredients on hand. Making sauces and condiments is far more economical that buying them at the store—and they are far better tasting.

Some of the recipes I have included are for making once a year from vegetables that are ready from the garden. Keep them on hand in the refrigerator to be used as you like throughout the year.

Barbecue Sauce

Makes 5½ cups—enough to fill one empty 44-ounce ketchup bottle. Prep time: 1 hour.

Store this sauce in the refrigerator; it will keep for up to a year. This mild sauce is very popular and can be used with beef, pork, or chicken.

¾ cup ketchup

¾ cup white vinegar

½ cup (1 stick) butter

¾ cup Worcestershire sauce

¾ cup fresh lemon juice

⅓ cup prepared mustard

1 tablespoon iodized salt

3 tablespoons paprika

3 tablespoons Hungarian paprika

2 tablespoons chili powder

2 teaspoons cayenne pepper

1 teaspoon ground cinnamon

1 cup dark molasses

1 cup packed dark brown sugar

4 cloves garlic, minced

¼ cup minced shallot

1. Mix ingredients together in a large saucepan; stir and simmer for about 30 minutes, until sauce has thickened and turned a darker color.

2. Let cool slightly then puree half of the sauce at a time in a blender until smooth. (This step can be omitted if you do not mind bits of garlic and shallots in the sauce.)

3. The sauce is now ready to use, or you can store it in a sealed glass jar or an empty 44-ounce ketchup bottle in the refrigerator.

4. To use for grilling, first sear meat at a high temperature then reduce heat before applying sauce. This will help prevent burning.

5. To use as a dipping sauce, heat sauce and either pour into individual serving dishes or pass the saucepan around the table with a ladle.

Chow-Chow Relish

Makes 5 cups. Prep time: 1 hour on day one, ½ hour on day two, and 10 minutes day three.

This recipe is a good way to use up end-of-the season garden vegetables. It's great as a relish for hot dogs or hamburgers or as a side to fish and chips.

1 small head green cabbage, outer leaves removed

1 green bell pepper

1 red bell pepper

1 green chili such as an Anaheim

1 red chili such as cayenne or Biggie

1 small carrot

1 medium yellow onion

1 large ripe tomato, peeled

1 green tomato (or 2 tomatillos if green tomatoes are not available)

1 clove garlic

¼ cup pickling salt

1 cup apple cider vinegar

½ cup brown sugar

1 teaspoon celery seed

1 teaspoon mustard seed

½ teaspoon ground black pepper

½ teaspoon ground cinnamon

½ teaspoon ground dry yellow mustard

½ teaspoon turmeric

¼ teaspoon ground cloves

¼ teaspoon ground ginger

1. Finely slice cabbage and cut slices crosswise to maximum width of ½ inch. Place in a large mixing bowl.

2. Finely dice next 8 vegetables (up to garlic clove) and add to chopped cabbage.

3. Using a garlic press, press garlic clove into diced vegetables.

4. Add pickling salt, stir, cover bowl with plastic wrap, and refrigerate overnight.

5. The next day, drain liquid in the bowl using cheesecloth or a colander. Liquid can be used in soup. You should have about 5 cups of chopped vegetables.

6. Add remaining ingredients, stir, cover with plastic wrap, and refrigerate overnight.

7. On third day, using cheesecloth or a colander, drain liquid and discard all but 1 cup.

8. Pack chow-chow relish with 1 cup of liquid in a glass jar with a screw lid and refrigerate. Chow-chow relish can be stored in refrigerator for up to 6 months.

Hamburger Sauce

Makes enough for 4 hamburgers. Prep time: 5 minutes.

Spread this tasty sauce liberally on toasted hamburger buns, hot dog buns, or on other sandwiches. Refrigerate any unused amounts.

⅓ cup mayonnaise

⅓ cup finely chopped dill pickle

⅓ cup finely chopped yellow onion

2 tablespoons steak sauce (I use Heinz 57)

1 teaspoon hot mustard

½ teaspoon ground black pepper

½ teaspoon iodized salt

1. Combine all ingredients and mix thoroughly.

Horseradish

Makes 1 quart. Prep time: 1 hour.

This mixture is pungent, so be careful smelling or breathing the vapors when making. I grind mine outside for that reason. Horseradish can be easily grown in the garden. Two or three plants will have enough roots for this recipe. Harvest the roots after frost in the fall but before the ground freezes.

4 cups diced horseradish root

2 cups white vinegar

1 teaspoon canning and pickling salt

1. Dig roots up (they grow deep, sometimes up to 12 inches) and wash well to remove dirt.

2. Save two or three root crowns and replant for next year's crop.

3. Peel remaining roots, both large and small, removing all skin and discoloration.

4. Slice and dice cleaned roots into ¼-inch diced pieces to make grinding easier.

5. Transfer pieces to a food processor with steel cutting blade.

6. Add vinegar and salt and process for about 5 minutes, wiping down sides of bowl occasionally.

7. Place mixture in a quart-sized glass jar with a tight lid and store in refrigerator.

Horseradish Sauce

Serves 6. Prep time: about 5 minutes.

OK to make ahead. This is a great sauce to serve with any roasted meat or on hamburgers. I use it primarily when I serve Beef Rib Roast Au Jus (page 103).

½ cup mayonnaise

2 tablespoons prepared mustard or try my Mustard (page 174)

¼ cup horseradish or try my Horseradish (page 172)

¼ cup whipped dessert topping

1. In a small bowl, mix all ingredients except whipped topping together until blended.

2. Fold in whipped topping.

3. Refrigerate until ready to use.

Mustard

Makes 2½ cups. Prep time: 9 days total (mostly waiting).

This is pungent mustard, so be careful smelling or breathing the vapors when making it. This makes a delicious popular Christmas gift. For more information on growing your own seed, see "mustard seed" in "Seasoning Your Food: Herbs, Spices, and Aromatics" (page 211).

1 cup brown mustard seeds

¾ cup apple cider vinegar

¾ cup amber German beer (preferably Märzen)

3 cloves garlic, pressed

1 tablespoon Worcestershire sauce

2 teaspoons canning and pickling salt

½ teaspoon turmeric

½ teaspoon paprika

1. In a stainless steel bowl, combine mustard seeds, vinegar, beer, and garlic. Cover and refrigerate for 48 hours.

2. After 48 hours, transfer bowl mixture to food processor with steel cutting blade and add remaining ingredients.

3. Process 3 to 4 minutes or more, until mixture turns to a creamy consistency.

4. The mixture may be slightly runny but will thicken as it ages.

5. Place mixture in a glass jar with a tight lid and keep in refrigerator.

6. Mustard is ready to use in 1 week; it will keep, refrigerated, for up to 1 year.

Salsa

Makes 5 pints. Prep time: about 1 hour.

This recipe is similar to the salsa recipe at www.mrswages.com and uses Mrs. Wages Classic Salsa Tomato Mix, a dry blend of dehydrated vegetables, salt, and spices. In addition to serving this salsa with corn chips, you will find that I use it in some dishes such as Vegetable Beef Soup (page 44).

6 pounds fresh tomatoes (about 20 medium)

1 cup finely chopped yellow onion

½ cup apple cider vinegar

1 (4 ounce) package Mrs. Wages Classic Salsa Tomato Mix

1. Wash tomatoes and, in batches, scald for 1 to 3 minutes in boiling water to loosen skins.

2. Using a slotted spoon, lift from boiling water and place in ice water to cool tomatoes quickly, until they can be handled.

3. Cut out tomato cores (where stem attaches), remove skins, and coarsely chop into a large pot. (You should have about 5 pints of tomatoes and juice after coring and skinning tomatoes.)

4. Add onions, vinegar, and salsa mix.

5. Bring to a boil over medium heat, stirring occasionally.

6. Reduce heat and simmer for 10 minutes.

7. Let cool and refrigerate for immediate use, or place into pint containers and freeze for later use.

Shrimp Cocktail Sauce

Makes enough for 8 to 10 shrimp cocktails, or enough to fill one 12-ounce chili sauce bottle.
Prep time: 10 minutes.

Shrimp cocktails can provide a great first course to your dinner. I make mine in 4.5 ounce sherbet cups by first finely shredding lettuce to provide a bed to receive the cooked shrimp which is topped with this sauce. Enjoy!

1 (12 ounce) bottle chili sauce (I use Heinz)

1 teaspoon Worcestershire sauce

1 tablespoon prepared horseradish

½ teaspoon iodized salt

½ teaspoon freshly ground white pepper

½ cup finely minced celery heart

Dash or two of hot pepper sauce, to taste

1. Mix all ingredients together in a small bowl and refrigerate.

2. Use as a topping for shrimp cocktails.

3. Any leftover sauce can be saved by using a funnel to refill empty chili sauce bottle; refrigerate for up to 2 months.

Tartar Sauce

Serves 6. Prep time: about 5 minutes.

It is OK to make the tartar sauce the day before to accompany dishes such as Fish and Chips (page 100), hamburgers, or salmon burgers.

1 cup mayonnaise

½ cup finely diced dill pickle

1 tablespoon finely chopped fresh parsley

¼ cup finely chopped yellow onion

1 tablespoon hot mustard (or try my Mustard, page 174)

½ teaspoon hot sauce (I use Tabasco)

½ teaspoon ground black pepper

1. In a small bowl, mix all ingredients together until blended.

2. Refrigerate until ready to use. The tartar sauce will keep, refrigerated, for about 2 weeks.

Pickling and Fermenting

Pickling and fermenting have been used for centuries as ways to preserve foods. In the summer and fall months, pickling and fermenting were used to preserve vegetables from the garden so they could be enjoyed in the winter and early spring, when fresh vegetables were not available. Making your own pickles provides superior-tasting pickles and interesting gifts. There are many different types of pickles that can be made. This cookbook contains a few recipes that I've have used, including one for sauerkraut.

You can pickle vegetables and keep them in the refrigerator for a month or two; if you want to keep pickles longer, canning in boiling water is necessary. If you are not familiar with canning, consult USDA Bulletin 539, 1994 edition (or more current edition) available from the National Center for Home Food Preservation website at http://www.uga.edu/nchfp/publications/publications_usda.html.

Other good sources of information are www.homecanning.com. and the Mrs. Wages Home Canning Guide available at www.mrswagesstore.com. These references have modern, safe recipes for many types of pickles. You will need a boiling water canner made of porcelain enamel steel, aluminum, or stainless steel that will hold seven quart jars. (I use a thirty-quart liquid capacity stainless steel pot with a lid, which I also use for making beer.) You'll also need a timer, a jar rack, a jar lifter, and a way to heat the water in the canner, since most modern home stoves won't be up to the task. (I use a 60,000 BTU outdoor propane burner.)

Never use old recipes for pickling or canning, as they can be deadly. The bacteria that exist today did not exist years ago when your grandmother made pickles. Methods have changed and boiling water processing times have been increased to prevent botulism. Processing times also increase with altitude, so processing times at sea level are shorter than times at higher elevations. It is very important to follow the canning procedures exactly for success and safety. Canned pickles are best if used within one year. When opening jars of canned pickles, always make sure the lid was sealed and the liquid is not cloudy, slimy, or odorous; if you notice any of these conditions, discard the pickles.

Last, good water and high-quality produce are necessary for making good pickles. If your tap water is hard, cloudy, or odorous, then use bottled or filtered water. Also make sure that your vegetables are freshly picked, and not rotted or soft. Use pickling cucumbers as they are bred for pickling. Cleanliness, including jar sterilization, is also very important.

I hope I have not scared you away from pickling and fermenting with all of the above information. I realize that learning to can pickles takes some learning, but once you figure it out, the process becomes almost automatic, so I would encourage you to tough it out. Why? Because the effort pays off with great-tasting results and you will always have fond memories of the pickling brine smell in your kitchen.

Bread and Butter Pickles

Makes 7 quarts. Prep time: 3 hours, using a boiling water canner.

This is a recipe from Mrs. Wages (made by Precision Foods), and it uses Mrs. Wages Quick Process Bread & Butter Pickle Mix. Please read the introduction to this section on page 179 before proceeding. You will note that I use the pickles and pickle juice from this recipe in my Potato Salad (page 33) and Pasta Salad (page 31).

9 to 11 pounds of fresh, firm pickling cucumbers 4 to 6 inches long. Note: You may not be able to get all of these cucumbers into the jars, so I do not slice them all until I complete packing the jars to prevent having unused slices.

6¾ cups distilled white vinegar (5 percent acidity)

7 cups granulated sugar

1 (5.3 ounce) pouch bread and butter pickle mix. (I use *Mrs. Wages Quick Process Bread & Butter Pickle Mix*)

7 large-mouth one-quart canning jars (check to be sure they are not cracked or chipped)

7 new large-mouth canning jar lids (never reuse canning jar lids)

7 large-mouth canning jar lid rings (can be reused if not rusty)

1. Wash quart jars in hot soapy water and thoroughly rinse, or run them through dishwasher.

2. Wash cucumbers and cut off stems and blossom ends. In a large bowl, slice unpeeled cucumbers into ⅛-inch-thick rounds. (I use a crinkle-cut garnishing tool to cut cukes to add interest.)

3. Fill canner with about 18 gallons water; it needs to be at least 1 inch above quart jars. Start burner to heat water to boiling. This will take 15 to 20 minutes. Insert canning rack into canner and, using jar lifter, lower each empty quart jar into water. Make sure water is 1 inch above the now filled-with-water jars. Cover pot with lid; wait for water to reach a rapid boil then boil for 10 minutes to sterilize jars.

4. While canner water with jars is rapidly boiling, mix together vinegar, sugar, and pickle mix in a large stainless steel or porcelain pot (do not use aluminum); heat and stir until mixture just begins to boil. Reduce heat to low but keep liquid hot.

5. Wash jar lids and rings in hot soapy water and rinse. Place lids in another pot with water and heat, but do not boil. Reduce heat to low but keep water hot.

6. After the 10 minutes of jar sterilization has elapsed, use jar lifter to remove jars, draining their contained water back into canner. Set hot jars upright on a clean towel. The jars are now sterile and ready to fill.

7. In each sterile jar, pack cucumber chips tightly.

8. Add enough hot solution of vinegar, sugar, and pickle mix to fill each quart jar to within ½ inch of jar top.

9. Wipe jar rim with a clean, damp paper towel to remove any hot solution.

10. Place hot jar lids onto jar tops and secure lid with ring to finger tight. Do not overtighten lids.

11. Using jar lifter, slowly (to avoid cracking jar) lower filled jars into canner. The top of the water should be at least 1 inch above the top of the jars. If not, add water.

12. Allow water to return to a rapid boil then process (boil) for 10 minutes for altitudes 0 to 1,000 feet. At altitudes of 1,000 feet or more, increase processing time 1 minute for each 1,000 feet in elevation.

13. At the end of the processing time, remove jars from canner using jar lifter, and place on a clean towel. Do not touch lids. As jars cool, lids will pop and go from convex to concave, meaning the lid has sealed. If a jar fails to seal within 30 minutes, the jar is not sealed and must be refrigerated and used right away.

14. After jars are cool, you can remove lid rings and reuse them or leave rings in place.

15. Mark lid with year and batch number and store in a cool area out of sunlight.

16. These are ready to open and eat in 2 days.

Dill Pickles

Makes 7 quarts. Prep time: 2 to 2½ hours, using a boiling water canner.

Please read the introduction to this section (page 179) before proceeding. Homemade dill pickles are delicious served as a side or sliced on hamburgers.

15 pounds of fresh pickling cucumbers (35 to 40 cucumbers, each 3 to 5 inches long)

6½ cups apple cider vinegar (5 percent acidity)

6½ cups water (use bottled/filtered water if your tap water is hard or tastes bad)

2 tablespoons sugar

¼ cup canning and pickling salt (do not use plain, iodized, or kosher salt)

7 large stems of fresh dill, with flower heads

14 cloves garlic, peeled and cut in half

4 jalapeño or other hot peppers, cut in half

14 black peppercorns

7 teaspoons yellow mustard seed

1 (26 gram) packet calcium chloride (I use Ball Pickle Crisp)

7 wide-mouth quart canning jars (check to be sure they are not cracked or chipped)

7 new wide-mouth canning jar lids (never reuse canning jar lids)

7 wide-mouth canning jar rings (can be reused if not rusty)

1. Wash quart jars in hot soapy water and thoroughly rinse or run them through dishwasher.

2. Wash cucumbers and cut off blossom ends and leave short stems on.

3. Fill canner with about 24 quarts water; it needs to be at least 1 inch above the quart jars. Start burner to heat water to boiling. This will take 15 to 20 minutes. Insert canning rack into canner and, using jar lifter, lower each empty quart jar into water. Make sure water is 1 inch above the now filled-with-water jars. Cover canner with lid; wait for water to reach a rapid boil then boil for 10 minutes to sterilize jars.

4. While canner water with jars is rapidly boiling, mix together vinegar, water, sugar, and salt in a large stainless steel or porcelain pot (do not use aluminum); heat, stirring, until mixture begins to boil. Reduce heat to low but keep liquid hot. (Remove pot from heat just as boil begins.)

5. Wash jar lids and rings in hot soapy water and rinse. Place lids in another pot with water and heat, but do not boil. Reduce heat to low but keep water hot.

6. After the 10 minutes of jar sterilization has elapsed, use jar lifter to remove jars, draining their contained water back into canner. Set hot jars upright on a clean towel. The jars are now sterile and ready to fill.

7. In each sterile jar, place 1 head of dill, 2 garlic clove halves, half a jalapeño pepper, 2 peppercorns, 1 teaspoon mustard seed, and 1 ½ teaspoons calcium chloride.

8. Pack cucumbers tightly in quart jar in an upright position.

9. Add enough hot vinegar solution to fill each quart jar to within ½ inch of top.

10. Wipe jar rim with a clean, damp paper towel to remove any hot solution.

11. Place hot jar lids onto jar tops and secure lid to finger tight. Do not overtighten lids.

12. Using jar lifter, slowly (to avoid cracking jar) lower filled jars into canner. The top of the water should be at least 1 inch above the top of the jars. (You probably will need to remove some of the canner water.)

13. Allow water to return to a rapid boil then process (boil) for 15 minutes for altitudes 0 to 1,000 feet; 20 minutes for 1,000 1to 6,000 feet; and 25 minutes above 6,000 feet.

14. At the end of the processing time, remove jars from canner using jar lifter and place on a clean towel. Do not touch lids. As jars cool, lids will pop and go from convex to concave, meaning the lid has sealed. If a jar fails to seal within one-half hour, the jar is not sealed and must be refrigerated and used right away.

15. After jars are cool, you can remove lid rings and reuse them or leave rings in place.

16. Mark lid with year and batch number and store in a cool area out of sunlight.

17. These will be ready to open and eat in 2 weeks.

Pickled Dilled Beans

Makes 7 pints. Prep time: 2 to 2½ hours, using a boiling water canner.

Please read the introduction to this section (page 179) before proceeding. I serve these as an appetizer all the time since everyone enjoys them.

5 pounds fresh tender green and or yellow beans or a mix of both, preferably straight and mostly 5 to 6 inches long

4 cups distilled white vinegar (5 percent acidity)

4 cups water (use bottled water if your tap water is hard or tastes bad)

¼ cup canning and pickling salt (do not use plain, iodized, or kosher salt)

7 large stems of fresh dill, with flower heads

7 cloves garlic, peeled and cut in half

4 jalapeño or other hot peppers, cut in half

7 regular pint canning jars (wide mouth jars are shorter and do not work as well, but can be used with beans cut to a 3¾-inch length)

7 new regular pint canning jar lids (never reuse canning jar lids)

7 regular pint canning jar rings (can be reused if not rusty)

1. Check to be sure jars are not cracked or chipped then wash pint jars in hot soapy water and thoroughly rinse or run them through dishwasher.

2. Wash beans, remove stem ends, and cut beans into 4-inch lengths. You should have 3½ pounds of 4-inch-long beans, and about 1½ pounds of cut-up beans that are shorter. (The shorter pieces can be blanched and frozen, or cooked fresh.)

3. Fill canner with about 18 quarts of water; it needs to be at least 1 inch above the pint jars. Start burner to heat water to boiling. This will take 15 to 20 minutes. Insert canning rack into canner and using jar lifter, lower each empty pint jar into water. Make sure water is 1 inch above the now filled-with-water jars. Cover with lid and wait for rapid boil to start and then boil for 10 minutes to sterilize jars.

4. While canner water with jars is rapidly boiling, mix together vinegar, water, and salt in a large stainless steel or porcelain pot (do not use aluminum) and heat, stirring, until mixture begins to boil. Reduce heat to low but keep liquid hot. (Remove pot from heat just as boil begins.)

5. Wash jar lids and rings in hot soapy water and rinse. Place lids in another pot with water and heat but do not boil. Reduce heat to low but keep water hot.

6. After the 10 minutes of jar sterilization has elapsed, use jar lifter to remove jars, draining their contained water back into canner. Set hot jars upright on a clean towel. The jars are now sterile and ready to fill.

7. In each sterile jar, place 1 head of dill, 2 cloves garlic halves, and ½ jalapeño pepper.

8. Pack 4-inch-long beans tightly in pint jar in an upright position.

9. Add enough hot vinegar solution to fill each pint jar to within ½ inch of jar top.

10. Wipe jar rim with a clean, damp paper towel to remove any hot solution.

11. Place hot jar lids onto jar tops and secure lid with ring to finger tight. Do not overtighten lids.

12. Using jar lifter, slowly (to avoid cracking jar) lower filled jars into canner. The top of the water should be at least 1 inch above the top of the jars. If not, add water.

13. Allow water to return to a rapid boil then process (boil) for 5 minutes for altitudes 0 to 1,000 feet; 10 minutes for 1,000 to 6000 feet; and 15 minutes above 6,000 feet.

14. At the end of the processing time, remove jars from canner using jar lifter and place on a clean towel. Do not touch lids. As jars cool, lids will pop and go from convex to concave meaning the lid has sealed. If a jar fails to seal within half an hour, then the jar is not sealed and must be refrigerated and used right away.

15. After jars are cool, you can remove lid rings and reuse them or leave rings in place.

16. Mark lid with year and batch number and store in a cool area out of sunlight.

17. These will be ready to open and eat in 2 weeks.

Mustard Pickles

This recipe makes four 1-quart or one 1-gallon jar(s) of pickles. Prep time: 30 minutes, plus 3 to 4 days refrigeration time.

This is a very easy recipe since there is no canning, water bath, or hassle; you simply keep them in the refrigerator. These pickles are very tangy and so easy to make that in the 1950s Farm Journal Magazine called them "Lazy Wife Pickles," a title I felt would not be appropriate today! This is a good way to use extra cucumbers left over from canning, as you can add cucumbers to the jar at any time throughout the cucumber harvest. If you do not have the very small cucumbers, you can slice spears from larger ones—but in my opinion, they're not as good. You can also use green beans, small carrots, small onions, garlic, cauliflower, asparagus, or any combination thereof. These wonderful pickled vegetables will keep in the refrigerator for several months.

Enough very small pickling cucumbers to fill a gallon jar (You can start with fewer and add cucumbers as you harvest them.)

3 quarts apple cider vinegar

¾ cup canning and pickling salt (Do not use plain, iodized, or kosher salt.)

¾ cup dry mustard powder

1. Wash and dry cucumbers.

2. In a gallon jar, add vinegar, salt, and dry mustard; stir to mix. (If using 4 quart jars, divide ingredients equally among jars.)

3. Add cucumbers.

4. Make sure cucumbers are covered with liquid. If not, weigh them down using 2 pint-sized plastic freezer bags. Insert one inside the other and fill the inside bag with water; seal both bags and place in the gallon jar.

5. Keep gallon jar covered and refrigerated.

Pickled Red Beets

Serves 4 (about 4 cups). Prep time: 1 hour.

Pickled red beets are one of my favorite side dishes; they are easy to make and require no canning. Store them in a covered jar in the refrigerator for up to 3 months. To make larger amounts, increase all ingredients proportionally.

4 large red beets

½ cup apple cider vinegar

1 teaspoon canning and pickling salt (Do not use plain, iodized, or kosher salt.)

1 tablespoon sugar

½ cup water

½ small yellow onion, sliced

¼ stick cinnamon

1 whole clove

1. Trim off beet tops, leaving ½ inch of stems and root intact. Wash to remove all dirt.

2. Place beets in a large pot and cover with water.

3. Over medium-high heat, bring beets to a boil.

4. Cover and reduce heat to medium and cook for 30 minutes or until beets are fork-tender.

5. Drain beets, discarding liquid. Allow beets to cool so they can be handled.

6. Wash pot used to cook beets and add remaining 6 ingredients. Heat to just below boiling and reduce to simmer.

7. Peel beets and slice ¼-inch thick; add them to liquid in pot. (I use a crinkle-cut garnishing tool to slice the beets to add interest.)

8. Allow to simmer for 15 minutes, stirring occasionally.

9. Remove from heat; allow to cool somewhat. (Cooling lessens the chance of getting burned and avoids placing a hot item in the refrigerator.) Pour the beets and the liquid into a glass jar. Cover and refrigerate.

Sauerkraut

Makes 4 quarts. Prep time: 1 hour, plus 1 month to ferment.

Fall is a great time of year to make sauerkraut: the new crop of cabbage will be ready in the garden, and temperatures should be ideal for fermenting the cabbage—between 70 and 75 degrees F. But you can make sauerkraut anytime, using cabbage from the market. This sauerkraut is made in a 2-gallon crock (you could also use a 2-gallon stainless steel pot). You'll need something to "stomp" the cabbage in the crock. I made mine out of wood, but a quart jar filled with water with a lid works well, as you can hold it in your hand and stomp it up and down on the cabbage. Also needed is a way to weigh the cabbage down in the crock. I use two quart-sized plastic freezer bags: Insert one inside the other and fill the inside bag with water; seal both bags. Once fermented, the sauerkraut will keep in the refrigerator for 2 months. Sauerkraut contains lactic acid bacteria as well as vitamins and minerals that have health benefits. Homemade is much better tasting than the canned sauerkraut from the stores. It can be served hot as a side dish or hot or cold in sandwiches. Try making Reuben sandwiches using my Rye Dinner Rolls (page 159) with this sauerkraut for a real treat.

2 large heads of green cabbage (5 to 6 pounds total)

¼ cup canning and pickling salt (Do not use plain, iodized, or kosher salt.)

1. Discard outer green leaves of each head of cabbage or use in Stuffed Cabbage recipe (page 75).

2. Rinse each head and pat dry.

3. Cut each head through the core into quarters.

4. Cut core from each quarter and discard.

5. Shred cabbage into $1/16$- to ⅛-inch thick slices, using a knife or cabbage shredder.

6. When 2 of the quarters have been shredded, place it in crock and sprinkle with 1 tablespoon salt.

7. Mix cabbage and salt thoroughly with gloved hand.

8. "Stomp" this layer until juices are drawn out of cabbage.

9. Repeat steps 5 through 8 three additional times until all cabbage and salt are used.

10. When complete, juices should cover the cabbage by 1 to 2 inches. If not, add boiled and cooled brine to cover. (Brine is made by dissolving 1½ tablespoons pickling salt in 1 quart of water.)

11. Place water-filled plastic bag weight on top of cabbage and cover crock with a clean tea towel. (Using a tea towel allows gases from the fermenting process to escape without exploding.)

12. Monitor air temperature in the room where the crock is kept to maintain 70 to 75 degrees temperature. (In the fall, I find that this is easily accomplished in my kitchen, but your climate may be different.) Check crock periodically (and again at the end of 1 month) and skim off and dispose of any mold or slime.

13. At the end of the 1-month fermenting time, remove sauerkraut from crock and place in sterile glass jars with lids. Store in refrigerator for up to up to 2 months. (It never lasts that long.)

Beer, Wine, Punches, and Liqueurs

Making your own homemade beverages is not only fun, but very cost effective. It is legal in the United States to make small amounts of beer and wine for not-for-sale consumption—thanks to President Jimmy Carter—but check state and local laws, as a few do not allow the practice and many have restrictions.

Once you have the bottles and equipment you need, beer can be made for less than fifty cents per bottle, and wine in the two to three dollar range per bottle. Liqueurs are also very cost effective to make, and they make nice Christmas presents, too.

I am not including any beer or wine recipes, as they are readily available online or from the retail companies that sell beer- and wine-making supplies in your area. Remember to always use bottled water, as high chlorine, hard water, or off-tasting water will ruin your batch. The critical thing to remember in making both beer and wine is that sanitation and cleanliness are paramount to success. Be faithful about following the recipe directions, including all the sterilization and rinsing instructions. Ruining a five-gallon batch (because you were careless) means pouring what you made down the drain.

HOMEMADE BEER

I have made many different beers. I make lager in the winter so that I can allow the fermentation to occur at low temperatures without needing to make room in my refrigerator for a five-gallon carboy! The other varieties can be made anytime during the year. These are five-gallon batches generally so you will need about fifty eleven-ounce bottles that are made for regular (not twist-off) caps. You can buy new bottles, or save non-twist-off purchased beer bottles after they are empty. You will also need a thirty-quart stainless steel pot with a lid, and a way to heat it (I use a 60,000-BTU outdoor propane burner). You will need to buy a capper, fermenting vat, carboy, air lock, tubing, a hydrometer, and other miscellaneous items from your Internet or local home-brew supply store. They'll tell you what you need, and will also sell you all the actual ingredients, such as grains, hops, etc. Beer should be stored in a cool dark place; it will be ready to drink in about one month.

HOMEMADE WINE

How about serving your own wine with your next dinner? Your guests will appreciate the effort you went to in making the wine. Different varieties of wine can be made from some very good wine-making kits that include all the ingredients you need (available on the Internet or from your local wine-making supply store). You can also make wine from fruit and berries that you buy or grow yourself. If you have the equipment to make beer, you have most of the items you need to make wine except for a cork driver. You will need about twenty-four wine bottles per batch, which you can buy or save up. Wine bottles should be stored in a cool, dark place on their sides, so that the corks stay wet. The recipe will tell you when the wine can be consumed, but generally it will be from two months to a year, depending on the variety of wine.

HOMEMADE PUNCHES AND LIQUEURS

Homemade liqueurs make great Christmas gifts! I have included liqueur recipes that are easy to make. Buy the liquor you need in the 1.75-liter size to cut down on cost. If you want thicker, syrupy liqueurs (closer to the consistency of the ones you buy) add two teaspoons of food grade glycerin per quart of liqueur. Glycerin is available at beer- and wine- making supply stores, in some drug stores, or on the Internet.

Most of my punch recipes are nonalcoholic. For punch recipes that are mostly alcoholic, buy a used copy of *Trader Vic's Bartender's Guide*, which was first published in 1947—it's a classic.

Banana Punch

Serves 25 or enough for (25) 6-ounce cups. Prep time: 15 minutes.

Make this one day before serving to allow time for it to freeze.

6 ripe bananas

1 (12 ounce) can frozen lemonade concentrate, softened

2 (12 ounce) cans frozen orange juice concentrate, softened

2 (12 ounce) cans frozen pineapple juice concentrate, softened

5 liters lemon-lime soda, chilled

1. In a blender, add peeled bananas and juices; blend. (You may need to do this in batches, depending on the size of your blender.)

2. Into a large stainless steel mixing bowl that will nest inside your punch bowl, pour blended mixture. Freeze overnight.

3. When ready to serve, unmold frozen mixture by floating bowl briefly in hot water.

4. Place frozen round in punch bowl with rounded side up.

5. Add soda 30 minutes before serving.

Brunch Punch

Serves 25 or enough for (36) 6-ounce cups. Prep time: 10 minutes.

If you want to use an ice mold, make it ahead of time. It can be as simple as a round block of ice made in a small stainless steel mixing bowl. Be sure to thaw the frozen juice concentrates ahead of time to make mixing easier.

1 quart orange juice

1 (46 ounce) can pineapple juice

1 (6 ounce) can frozen lemonade concentrate, softened

1 (6 ounce) can frozen limeade concentrate, softened

2 quarts ice water

2 (2-liter) bottles chilled ginger ale

1 small ice mold or ice cubes

1. Mix fruit juices with water in punch bowl.

2. Just before serving, add ginger ale.

3. Add ice mold or cubes.

Champagne Punch

Serves 18 or enough for (18) 6-ounce cups. Prep time: 10 minutes.

Buy inexpensive champagne and save the more costly champagne for special occasions.

2 (750 ml) bottles of champagne

1 cup brandy

1 cup orange liqueur

1 (1-liter) bottle club soda, chilled

12 strawberries with stems removed, washed, and cut in half

1. Mix liquids in punch bowl.

2. Float strawberries on top.

3. Serve one strawberry piece with each serving.

Ice Cream Punch

Serves 25 or enough for (25) 6-ounce cups Prep time: 10 minutes.

This is a quick and easy punch to make for wedding receptions or open houses.

2 (6 ounce) cans frozen lemonade concentrate, softened

1 (6 ounce) can frozen orange concentrate, softened

9 cups water

1 quart lemon sherbet

1 quart vanilla ice cream

1. Mix fruit juices with water in punch bowl.

2. Scoop sherbet and ice cream into punch using a small melon baller; stir gently.

3. Serve a ball of ice cream and sherbet with each serving.

Coffee Liqueur

Makes 1½ quarts. Prep time: 1 hour, plus 1 week to mellow.

This is a wonderful after-dinner treat or a nice adult ice cream topping.

4 cups sugar

2 cups bottled water

1 cup instant coffee granules

1 tablespoon vanilla extract

1 bottle (750ml) cheap vodka

½ cup brandy

1. In a medium-sized pot, mix sugar and water; bring to a boil over medium heat, stirring to dissolve sugar.

2. Add coffee and vanilla. Turn off heat and stir until coffee dissolves.

3. Allow to cool completely to room temperature (otherwise, the alcohol will evaporate when added).

4. Add vodka and brandy, stir, and pour into clean glass bottles or jars, with clean lids.

5. This liqueur will keep for a long time—up to 1 year—if kept in a cool place (70 degrees F. maximum).

Orange Liqueur

Makes about 1 quart. Prep time: 1 hour, plus 2 to 3 weeks to mellow.

Serve this to adults as a topping over their favorite ice cream.

1 cup sugar

½ cup bottled water

2 teaspoons orange extract

3½ cups brandy

1. In a medium-sized pot, mix sugar and water and bring to a boil over medium heat, stirring to dissolve sugar.

2. Allow to cool completely to room temperature (otherwise, the alcohol will evaporate when added).

Irish Cream

Makes 3 cups. Prep time: 15 minutes.

This also makes a great after-dinner drink.

3 large eggs

3 tablespoons chocolate syrup

2 tablespoons vanilla extract

1 tablespoon instant coffee powder (I use Folgers Classic Roast instant coffee)

1 (13½ ounce) can sweetened condensed milk

1 cup heavy cream

2 cups Irish whiskey

1. In a blender, add eggs, syrup, vanilla, and coffee and blend.

2. Transfer to a large bowl and add remaining ingredients. Mix well.

3. Pour into clean glass bottles or jars with clean lids and seal. Store in refrigerator for up to 2 months.

Olio

This is where you will find recipes that were not suited for the other parts of this book. The Papier-Mâché Paste recipe is for craftwork and not eating! Remember that the difference between wallpaper paste and good gravy is salt and pepper.

Beef Jerky

Makes about 75 pieces. Prep time: 2 days.

This jerky can be made in the oven or in a food dehydrator. Buy the meat when it is on sale (freeze it if you can't use it right away) to keep the cost down. After drying, the jerky can be frozen for later use.

1½ pounds lean flank or round steak

¼ cup Worcestershire sauce

¼ cup soy sauce

1 tablespoon garlic juice, squeezed from garlic cloves

1 tablespoon onion juice, squeezed from a medium yellow onion

1 teaspoon iodized salt

1 teaspoon freshly ground black pepper

1. Partially freeze meat to aid in slicing it; if frozen, partially defrost.

2. Using a sharp knife, thinly slice meat at right angles to the grain of the meat.

3. Remove and discard fat from slices.

4. In a resealable plastic bag, mix remaining ingredients together to make a marinade.

5. Place sliced meat in bag and refrigerate for 24 hours or more, up to 3 days.

6. After marinating, remove beef slices and drain bag. Finish drying by patting with a clean cloth or paper towels.

7. Lay a catch pan of aluminum foil on bottom oven rack and then place slices on a clean upper oven rack or in dehydrator (you may also need a catch pan in dehydrator).

8. Set oven on lowest temperature setting (150 degrees F) or in dehydrator at 150 degrees F or as recommended by dehydrator manufacturer.

9. Allow jerky to dry for 4 to 6 hours or per dehydrator directions. It should be dried until it is chewy and flexible but not brittle.

10. 10. Keep dried jerky in a resealable plastic bag in refrigerator for up to 1 month or in freezer for 6 months.

Peanut Butter

Serves 8. Prep time: 10 minutes.

Use this recipe to make chunky-style peanut butter. Larger batches can be made by doubling the recipe or by making several batches, depending on the capacity of your blender. A food processor can also be used for larger amounts.

2¼ cups roasted, salted peanuts, with or without the red skins

1 tablespoon peanut oil

More iodized salt, if needed

1. In a blender, add 2 cups of peanuts and oil and blend until desired consistency is achieved. Add salt to taste.

2. Hand-chop remaining ¼ cup of peanuts and stir into blended peanut butter.

3. Place peanut butter in a glass jar with a lid and store in refrigerator.

4. If oil separates, stir before serving.

Roasted Nuts

Serves 8. Prep time: 30 minutes.

Use this recipe to roast any kind of raw nuts, including peanuts, walnuts, pecans, hazelnuts, and almonds. Raw peanuts can be purchased on the Internet since they can be hard to find in bulk (except in the South), but other raw nuts are available everywhere. All nuts used in this recipe are shelled. Seasoning can be as simple as salt, or you can spice them up by adding chili powder, cayenne pepper, seasoning salt, or garlic salt.

3 cups raw, shelled nuts

1 tablespoon peanut oil

Iodized salt or other seasoning

1. Preheat oven to 325 degrees F and set a rack in middle of oven.

2. Coat a shallow baking pan with oil.

3. Place a single layer of nuts in pan and place in preheated oven.

4. Roast for 15 to 20 minutes, stirring every 5 minutes until nuts are roasted to your liking. (Nuts are easy to burn so keep an eye on them in roasting process.)

5. Nuts will continue to cook after removal from oven, so take them out on the "green" side of being done.

6. Place nuts on paper towels to remove any oil.

7. Place nuts in a bowl and add salt or other seasonings to taste; stir to coat evenly.

8. Serve warm or allow to cool. Store at room temperature (up to 1 month) or freeze for later use.

Trail Mix

Serves 8. Prep time: 45 minutes.

Going on a hike? Take this along.

3 cups thick-rolled oats

½ cup wheat bran

½ cup margarine or butter, melted

½ cup honey

½ cup brown sugar

1 teaspoon vanilla extract

½ cup shredded unsweetened coconut

1 cup raisins

1 cup roasted almonds

1 cup roasted peanuts

1 cup plain candies (I use M&Ms.)

1 cup dried fruit (apples, pears, peaches, figs, or dates), cut into small pieces

1. Preheat oven to 300 degrees F.

2. In a medium mixing bowl, mix oats, wheat bran, margarine, honey, and brown sugar.

3. Spread mixture on a cookie sheet and bake in preheated oven for 30 minutes, stirring occasionally to redistribute.

4. Remove from oven and allow to cool completely.

5. Add remaining ingredients and stir to mix.

6. Place mixture in pint- or quart-sized plastic freezer bags. Freeze bags that will not be used immediately.

Papier-Mâché Paste

Makes 2½ cups. Prep time: 15 minutes.

Kids can make all kinds of things out of papier-mâché. Even though the process is somewhat messy, it is easy to clean up. This paste is economical and easy to make. Use strips of newspaper for the paper. When the artwork is finished and dry, paint with tempera paints.

¼ cup plus 2 tablespoons white flour

1 cup cold water

1 cup hot water

1 teaspoon iodized salt (to minimize molding)

1 teaspoon sugar (to make it smell better)

1. Mix flour with cold water until all lumps are dissolved.

2. In a small pan, heat hot water to boiling.

3. Slowly pour flour mix into boiling water while stirring.

4. Continue stirring for 5 minutes, until paste thickens.

5. To adjust paste consistency, add either water to thin or more flour/cold water to thicken.

6. Add salt and sugar, and stir to mix.

7. Allow to cool before using.

Seasoning Your Food: Herbs, Spices, and Aromatics

The following is a suggested list of herbs, spices, and aromatics that I recommend you keep on hand. In regard to the herbs and spices, a few not on this list may be required for certain recipes, but for the most part are rarely used. Always buy the smallest amount possible unless the item is used frequently, since herbs and spices lose potency with age.

HERBS

Many herbs can be grown in the garden or in pots on a windowsill or in a box on your patio or deck. Fresh herbs are more intense and provide superior flavor to those that are dried. If you grow your own herbs, use them fresh, or dry them by harvesting the plant stems with leaves before the plants go to seed. To dry, place stems loosely in a paper bag and set the bag in a dry warm area out of the sun to dry. Check the bag contents in one week to see of the leaves are crumbly dry. If not, continue drying until the leaves will easily crumble when handled. Remove the dried leaves, seal them in a glass jar, and store out of direct light to prevent color fading. Replace dried herbs yearly.

Common homegrown herbs include:

Basil: Basil is a tender annual that will need to be replaced each year from seed or from plants obtained from your local nursery. Basil requires warm weather and can be grown in pots. There are many different types of basil; the most common is sweet basil. To use, remove a few leaves at a time, wash if needed, and mince or use whole. Pinch off the tops of the plant to encourage growth and prevent the plant from going to seed. Basil is used to make delicious pesto and it is very popular in many dishes and noshes. Basil leaves remaining on the plant at the end of the season can be removed, washed if needed, and dried.

Bay Leaves: Bay leaves are harvested from the bay laurel tree, a slow-growing tree that can reach twelve feet in height—but which can easily be kept small by keeping it in a ten- to twelve-inch pot on your deck or patio. If the tree is potted, it should be brought inside during freezing weather to keep the roots from freezing. If planted in the ground, they are hardy to ten degrees F. To use the leaves, remove one leaf at a time, choosing a different branch each time a leaf is removed. Bay leaves are most often used in hearty, slow-cooked dishes such as soups, stews, and spaghetti sauce.

Chives: Chives are perennial and may be grown from seeds or obtained from your local nursery. They will overwinter in milder climates, such as the Pacific Northwest. At first frost, cut back to the ground and cover with mulch. Remove the mulch in early spring and enjoy them as one of the first green plants in early spring. They flower easily and the cheery purple flowers are also edible. To harvest chives, cut them off at ground level before they mature or go to seed; wash and remove lower part of the stalk. Mince and use as garnish in soups and other dishes. Several cuttings are possible from early spring to late fall if adequately watered. Mince chives before drying.

Cilantro: Cilantro is an annual and will need to be grown each year from seed or obtained as starts from your local nursery. Harvest the leaves to use in salsa and other dishes. The leaves can be dried but they do lose flavor. Let some of the cilantro plants go to seed: the very flavorful peppercorn-sized seed is called coriander, and is used in many dishes including soups and meat dishes. Collect the seeds when they are becoming dry on the plants but before they fall to the ground. Finish drying the seeds in a brown paper bag then store them in a glass bottle. The seed can be ground in a food blender or coffee grinder.

Dill: Dill is an annual and will need to be grown each year from seed, which easily germinates in the garden. If allowed to go to seed, the dill will re-seed itself for the next year. However, the dill may mature too early (common in many climates) to provide a supply for dill pickle canning. The early, "volunteer" dill may be used in soups and salads in the early spring when no other herbs are available. Plant more dill seed in June to early July for dill pickles. Let some go to seed, harvest the dried seeds, and place in a sealed glass jar. The seeds can be used in recipes and also used the next spring to plant in the garden. Green dill seed heads can be dried as well as frozen in freezer bags for use in canning.

Oregano: Oregano is a woody perennial, and should be bought from the nursery then planted in a pot or in the garden. There are several different kinds of oregano, but I prefer Greek or Italian oregano for cooking because of its pungent flavor. In the garden it is hardy to minus twenty degrees F. If in a pot, protect from very cold temperatures. Leaves can be removed as the plant grows and used fresh in pizza sauces, spaghetti, and other dishes. When the plant reaches ten inches in height and before it blooms, cut it off at the ground and dry the leafy stems for use year-round. The plants will re-grow and may require additional cutbacks throughout the summer.

Parsley: Parsley is a biennial, meaning it goes to seed in the second year and then dies, so it should be reseeded or replanted yearly. It can be planted from seed early in the spring or purchased as a plant from your local nursery. Italian (flat-leaf) and moss curled are the two common types. In the garden it is hardy to fifteen degrees F. If temperatures are lower, protect plants with mulch or blankets until warmer temperatures return. If planted in a pot, bring inside when temperatures are below freezing. Parsley can be used fresh in dishes and as garnish from early spring until it freezes in the fall. Remove aging stems to encourage more leafy growth.

Rosemary: Rosemary is a woody perennial and should be purchased from your local nursery then planted in a pot or in the garden. I prefer the prostrate variety. Remove the needles to use fresh in recipes. Since rosemary needles can be removed almost all year long, drying is not required unless you live in colder climates. To dry, remove twigs and dry and then remove needles before sealing in a glass jar. Rosemary plants will die at fifteen degrees F, so if temperatures that low are forecast, protect the plant by covering it with mulch, a blanket, or other protection. Remove the cover when temperatures rise again. If your rosemary plant is potted, bring it inside when temperatures are below freezing.

Sage: Sage is a woody perennial and should be purchased from your local nursery then planted in a pot or in the garden. Remove the leaves as needed to use fresh in recipes. Since sage leaves can be removed almost all year long, drying is not necessary unless you live in colder climates. Dry sage leaves on their branches then remove the leaves from the stems and place in a sealed glass jar. Sage plants will die at twenty degrees F, so if temperatures that low are forecast, protect the plant by covering it with mulch, a blanket, or other protection. Remove the cover when temperatures rise again. If your sage is in pots, bring it inside when temperatures are below freezing. Prune the tops to encourage bushy growth, and remove the seed stalks from the plant when they appear. Sage leaves are usually minced and used in sausage, and in turkey or chicken dishes and dressings.

Spearmint: Spearmint is a perennial, and once planted (typically as a plant from the nursery), will establish and spread to form many plants. For that reason, plant it in a container or other controlled spot to prevent it from taking over your whole garden! Spearmint starts growing early in the spring and should be harvested before the flowers form. When the plant reaches about ten inches in height, cut the stems off at the ground. Sprigs and leaves can be used as a garnish for drinks and desserts or dried for use as a tea. The spearmint will grow back after being cut off and may require additional cutbacks throughout the summer.

Tarragon: Tarragon is a perennial that can be grown in the garden from plants obtained from your local nursery. It is hardy to minus twenty degrees F, so if temperatures that low are forecast, protect the plant by covering it with mulch, a blanket, or other protection. Remove the cover when the temperatures rise again. If your tarragon is in pots, bring it inside when temperatures are below freezing. Tarragon is used primarily in meat dishes.

Thyme: Thyme is a woody perennial and should be purchased from your local nursery to plant in a pot or in the garden. Remove the leaves as needed to use fresh in recipes. Since thyme leaves can be harvested almost all year long, drying is not required unless you live in colder climates. To dry, cut the twigs at ground level before the plant blooms. When dry, remove the leaves from the twigs and seal in a glass jar. The thyme will re-grow after being cut off. Thyme plants will die at twenty degrees F, so if temperatures that low are forecast, protect the plant by covering it with mulch, a blanket, or other protection. Remove the cover when temperatures rise again. If your thyme is in pots, bring it inside when temperatures drop below freezing. Thyme is a versatile herb that goes with any meat and it is used in soups and Italian dishes, etc.

SPICES

Spices include those spices and seeds that can be purchased at the grocery store or in some cases, seeds that can be grown in the garden. Today we take spices for granted since they are readily available in grocery and specialty stores. Spices have been used for over five thousand years, dating back to the ancient Assyrians. Spice trade between Mediterranean Region and the Far East was occurring centuries before the peak of the Roman Empire. Spices were considered trading currency. The discovery of the Americas brought more spices to the European market. Thus as travel and trade became easier, spice use became available to more and more people in the world. Spices were a precious commodity and were often stolen or pilfered and for years the dock workers in London had their pockets sewn up to prevent them from stealing the spices they unloaded from ships! Today we are fortunate to easily obtain all the spices we need to add interest and flavoring to what we cook.

Common spices and seeds used for culinary purposes include:

Allspice: Allspice is from the Western Hemisphere. Available whole for use in soups, stews, and roasts, as well as for pickling. Ground allspice is commonly used in cakes, cookies, mincemeat, and ketchup.

Caraway Seed: Caraway seed is native to Europe. It is used whole and gives rye bread its distinctive taste.

Cayenne Pepper: Cayenne pepper is native to Central America and the West Indies. Cayenne peppers can be grown in the garden and used fresh or dried. To dry the peppers, use a dehydrator (unless you live in an area with hot, dry, late summer/fall weather where peppers can be dried outdoors). After drying, the peppers can be ground in a blender and sealed in a glass jar. Be careful when grinding to avoid inhaling! Cayenne pepper is used in Mexican dishes and to flavor (and add a kick to) stews, soup, and sausage.

Celery Seed and Celery Salt: Celery seed is native to the Mediterranean area and Central Asia. Celery salt is ground celery seed combined with salt. Both are used in many dishes including salad dressings and potato salad. Celery is a biennial plant, meaning it will form seed heads only during the second year of its life. Growing your own celery seed, considering how little is used, is usually not worth the effort for home gardeners.

Chili Powder: Chili powder is a mixture of ground red pepper, cumin, and oregano. It is primarily used in making chili.

Cinnamon: Cinnamon is grown in Southeast Asia and Indonesia, and is available in sticks or ground. It is used in cakes, pies, pastries, cereal, pickling, and as a seasoning for meat.

Cloves: Cloves are native to the Moluccas Islands (Spice Islands) in Indonesia. Available whole or ground. Whole cloves are used to stud baked hams and fruit; ground cloves are commonly used in baking and in savory sauces such as ketchup.

Cream of Tartar: Cream of tartar is potassium hydrogen tartrate. It helps stabilize and give more volume to beaten egg whites. It is also used to produce a creamier texture in candy and frosting.

Cumin: Cumin is native to the Mediterranean area. Generally used as a ground spice, it is used in Mexican dishes, stews, and soups.

Curry Powder: Curry powder originated in India and is a mix of several ground spices—therefore its flavors and level of heat can vary quite a lot. It is used, of course, in curry dishes as well as for additional color and flavor in things such as deviled eggs or Indian dishes.

Fennel Seed: Fennel seed is imported from India. It is a member of the anise family, and so has the flavor of licorice. Fennel seed can be used whole in soups, egg dishes, and salad dressings.

Ginger: Ginger comes from Southeast Asia and Jamaica. It can be grown indoors at home. It is available as whole ginger root and is used extensively in Asian or Indian dishes or dried and ground for use mainly in desserts like gingerbread.

Mace: Mace is also from the Moluccas Islands. Ground mace is used in cakes, custards, and for seasoning meats.

Mustard Seed: Mustard seed can be easily harvested from mustard plants grown in the garden. There are three types: white (mildly pungent) from the Mediterranean area, which actually looks yellow and is used to make prepared American-style mustard; brown (pungent) mustard from the Himalayas, which is used to make prepared mustard in Europe; and black (hot) from Asia Minor, which is mainly used in Indian cooking. Sow mustard seeds in early spring and thin plants to one foot apart. (Watch for aphids, as they love mustard when it blooms.) Harvest the seed stalks when seed pods develop a brownish color.

To process mustard seeds the Old World way, place the seed stalks in the sun and let them dry for two weeks then thresh out the seeds. Small amounts can be threshed by placing the seed stalks in an old pillowcase and walking on it to release the seeds. Discard the stalks and place the seeds and chaff in a bowl. With the help of a slight breeze, transfer the seeds and chaff from bowl to bowl until all the chaff is blown away and only the seed remains in the bowl. Store the seeds in an airtight jar. About twenty mustard plants will yield enough seed to make a quart of prepared mustard (see my recipe for Mustard, page 174, for making prepared mustard using brown mustard seeds). Whole mustard seed is used in pickles, corned beef, and relishes.

Nutmeg: Nutmeg also comes from the Moluccas Islands. Ground nutmeg is used in eggnog, to season meats, in custard dishes such as quiche, and in baking.

Paprika: Paprika is a pepper native to Central America. Ground paprika is used primarily as a colorful garnish for deviled eggs, potato salad, and casseroles.

Pepper: Pepper is native to the East Indies. It is the berry of a climbing vine, and is the most widely used spice in the world. There are two primary types: white and black. Both are available ground or whole. Grinding your own pepper, either coarse or fine, provides intense flavor and is recommended over buying ground pepper. White pepper is generally used in white sauces.

Poppy Seed: Poppy seed is native to southwestern Asia. The seed is from the opium poppy, but has no narcotic properties. It is used whole in muffins, other baked goods, and often in salad dressings.

Poultry Seasoning: Poultry seasoning is a blend of ground herbs. It is primarily used to season stuffing (dressing) in pork chops and fowl.

Pumpkin Pie Spice: Pumpkin pie spice is a ground blend of cinnamon, ginger, allspice, nutmeg, and cloves. It is used primarily in pumpkin pies.

Sesame Seed: Sesame seed is native to Asia. It is used whole or ground, both toasted and untoasted. To toast, place in a 325-degree F oven for ten minutes or until lightly brown. (Keep an eye on them as they toast to prevent burning.) Sesame seed is sprinkled on bread and rolls, and is used in candy and Asian dishes.

Turmeric: Turmeric is obtained from the root of a plant in the ginger family, and is native to China. It is an ingredient in curry powder and prepared mustard. Turmeric is used to add color and flavor to pickles, rice dishes, and soups.

Vanilla Extract: Vanilla extract is native to Mexico and Central America. It is the fruit of an orchid plant. Imitation vanilla is not made from these plants (it's actually the byproduct of paper products!) and does not have the same intensity or flavor. Vanilla extract is used mainly in desserts.

THE AROMATICS: ONIONS, LEEKS, SHALLOTS, GARLIC, AND HORSERADISH

"Aromatics," or the foods used across almost every cuisine to add depth and a base of flavor to many dishes, are essential to our everyday cooking. They flavor almost every savory dish in this cookbook. You cannot cook without them. Onions, leeks, shallots, garlic, and horseradish can all be grown in your garden; consult gardening books, websites, or seed catalogs for details on planting, growing, and harvesting these plants. Some are planted in the fall for harvest the next summer, so if you are thinking about growing any of these, be sure to understand the growing cycle and plan one year in advance.

Onions

Onions are used fresh and cooked in many dishes and for this reason, growing onions in the garden makes sense. Onions are very hardy and are easy to grow but they need lots of nitrogen and water. They are generally not bothered by insects or disease, provided you practice crop rotation and strict sanitation practices.

Common onion types include:

Bunching Onions or Scallions: These are the green onions you buy in the store to eat raw or to sprinkle, minced onto dishes such as nachos. They are planted from seed. For an early crop, seed heavily in a pot or container indoors in February or March and place under a grow light or windowsill. When the weather improves, separate the onions and plant in the garden when they are about six inches high. Transplanted scallions will be ready for use in the kitchen in early summer. Alternatively, bunching onions can be seeded directly in the garden in spring after the weather has warmed and the danger of frost has past. The directly seeded onions will be ready to harvest in six weeks. Plant another crop in August for harvesting in the fall. If frost is forecast, cover the onions with plastic. It is possible to keep green onions in the garden throughout the winter in milder climates.

Storage and Sweet Onions: Storage and sweet onions are the large yellow, white, or red onions that are sliced and used raw or cooked and added to many dishes. There are many varieties of storage and sweet onions, but they fall into four main types: long day, short day, day neutral, and intermediate day. If you live north of 36 degrees north latitude (Arkansas northern border or Las Vegas, Nevada) then you plant long-day varieties. If you live south of that line, you plant short-day varieties. Day-neutral and intermediate-day varieties can be planted in any location.

Both storage and sweet onions can be planted from seed in the garden, from onion sets (small dry onions), or from small green onion plants grown in milder climates in the winter and shipped for transplanting. Onions planted from sets tend to bolt (go to seed) more quickly than direct-sown seed or transplants—if this happens, the bulb is of no use—so pull it and enjoy using the onion. Note that as they mature, onion bulbs protrude from the ground; this is natural, and they should not be covered with soil. The onions are ready to pull when the stalks fold over. Allow the onions to dry in the sun, keeping any dew or rain off them until the stalks are dry (about two weeks). Cut off the stalks leaving ¾ inch from the bulb and any remaining roots and store them in mesh bags in a dry well-ventilated area at forty-five degrees F. (I use an old refrigerator.) Stored properly, sweet onions will keep for three months and storage types will keep until late next spring. Carefully follow the growing, harvesting, and storage guidelines found in the instructions shipped with your onion plants, or in seed catalogs, gardening books, or on websites.

Multiplier Onions: Multiplier onions produce a cluster of bulbs underground from a single planted bulb. The small one-inch-diameter bulbs can be peeled and used in dishes as a substitute for storage onions. They are planted in the fall with the top of the bulb at the surface of the ground and will be ready to harvest in July. Save a few bulbs to plant that fall for next year's crop. They can be grown in a container or pot.

Walking Onions: Walking onions, or Egyptian walking onions, are very hardy perennials. They form several small, pungent bulbs underground, and produce a cluster of red spicy bulbs at the top of the stems in lieu of flowers. Both the underground bulbs and stem bulbs can be used even though they are small. The stem bulbs are great pickled or used in pickling other garden veggies. In the winter, if the soil is kept from freezing by mulch or cover, the green stems and underground bulbs can be used as green onions when no other fresh onions are available in the garden. In the fall, the underground bulbs should be dug up, separated, and dried. Replant single bulbs in the fall for next year's crop. Walking onions are a good choice if you have little garden space.

Leeks

Leeks are a non-bulb-forming substitute for onions, but have their own mild yet distinctive flavor and beautiful color. Cream of leek soup is always a winter favorite. Leeks are a very hardy biennial, but are often grown as an annual from seed or transplants. They will provide fresh green onions throughout the winter and into spring if mulched to keep the ground unfrozen. They also need lots of nitrogen and water in well-drained, deeply composted soil; they're generally not bothered by insects or disease, provided you practice crop rotation and strict sanitation practices.

Shallots

Shallots produce a cluster of small bulbs underground from a single planted bulb. The bulbs, which are often split into two or three large "cloves," are peeled, cut, and used to add interesting flavor to dishes and sauces (as storage and sweet onions are) but with a more delicate taste preferred in preparing delicate sauces. They are planted in the fall with the top of the bulb at the surface of the ground and will be ready to harvest in July. They can be grown in a container or pot. They require lots of nitrogen and water. Cut off any seed pods if they emerge from the stems. Shallots are ready to pull when the tops lay over. Allow the shallots to dry in the sun, keeping any dew or rain off of them until the stalks are dry (about two weeks). Cut off the tops and any remaining roots, and store them in mesh bags in a dry-ventilated area at forty-five degrees F. (I use an old refrigerator.) Save a few bulbs to plant that fall for next year's crop. Stored properly, some shallots can be kept for nearly a year. Carefully follow growing, harvesting and storage procedures found in instructions shipped with your bulbs or in seed catalogs or on websites. Shallots are very easy to grow.

Garlic

Garlic is a very common ingredient in many dishes because the flavor it adds is unmistakable, unique, and enjoyable to eat. Fresh garlic is far superior in flavor to garlic powder or flakes. It is easy to grow in the garden and has few pests, and as long as it is watered regularly and gets plenty of nitrogen, it will grow in almost any soil. Garlic bulbs are planted in the fall before the ground freezes and will grow all winter, with the harvest in July. Cut off any seed pods if they emerge from the stems. The garlic bulb is ready to pull when the tops lay over. Allow the bulbs to dry in the sun, keeping any dew or rain off them until the stalks are dry (about two weeks). Cut off the tops and any remaining roots and store them in mesh bags in a dry well-ventilated area at forty-five degrees F. (I use an old refrigerator.) Stored properly, some garlic can be kept for nearly a year. Carefully follow growing, harvesting, and storage procedures found in instructions shipped with your bulbs, or in seed catalogs, in gardening books, or on websites.

Common garlic types include:

Hardneck: Hardneck garlic produces five to ten cloves per head and offers a high-quality garlic flavor. It does not keep as well as softneck garlic, however. Seed catalogs offer many varieties but I grow Spanish Roja, which is my favorite.

Softneck: Softneck garlic produces six to eighteen cloves per head. It keeps better than the hardneck and is the type you often see braided. Softneck garlic is also available in many varieties.

Elephant: Elephant garlic is more closely related to a leek. Its flavor is mild, and it produces five to seven cloves per head.

Horseradish

Horseradish is a perennial that must be planted in a contained area to prevent it from spreading throughout the garden. A section of root is planted in the fall or spring in well-drained, deeply composted soil. Dig up the roots in late fall after a frost, replanting a section of root for next year. Horseradish is very pungent, so avoid breathing its vapors when preparing horseradish. To make horseradish paste, see Horseradish (page 172). If you prefer a milder sauce, mix the horseradish root pieces with an equal amount of rutabaga or turnip and then process with vinegar. Horseradish is most commonly used as a condiment to prime rib or roast beef.

What Else to Keep on Hand

Here are my suggestions for the foods and condiments you should stock in your refrigerator, freezer, and in your cupboards or pantry for everyday use. You do not need to go out and buy all these items at once. Use these lists to help in stocking up. Also see the "Seasoning Your Food: Herbs, Spices, and Aromatics" section of this book for stocking those items. There are other items that you will end up adding for your individual needs and for unique menu items such as steak sauces and specialty teas.

What to Stock in the Refrigerator

Butter

Cheeses

Chili Sauce

Cottage Cheese

Fresh Fruit (most)

Fresh Meat

Fresh Vegetables

Half-and-Half

Horseradish

Hot Pepper Sauce (opened)

Jams and Jellies (opened)

Ketchup (opened)

Lunch Meat

Margarine

Mayonnaise (opened)

Milk

Molasses (opened)

Mustard (yellow, Dijon, whole grain)

Olives (black, stuffed green)

Parmesan Cheese (opened)

Peanut Butter

Pickles (bread and butter, dill)

Salad Dressings (opened)

Shortening (opened)

Soy Sauce (opened)

Yeast

What to Stock in the Freezer

Berries

Coffee

Flax seed (unopened)

Flours (unopened)

Fruits (dried or fresh)

Ice Cream

Meats

Nuts

Soups (frozen)

Vegetables (frozen)

What to Stock in Cupboard or Pantry

Baking Powder

Baking Soda

Beans (pinto, white, kidney)

Beef Broth (canned)

Bread Crumbs

Cake Mixes

Cereal (cold)

Cereal (hot)

Chicken Broth (canned)

Chilies (canned)

Clams (canned)

Cocoa

Coffee (regular, decaf)

Cornmeal (yellow)

Cornstarch

Crackers (saltine)

Crackers (snack)

Flax Seed (ground)

Flour (all-purpose, whole wheat)

Fruit (canned)

Fruit Cocktail (canned)

Honey

Gelatin Mix (various flavors)

Lentils (dried)

Meat (canned)

Mushrooms (canned)

Oatmeal (steel cut, thick rolled)

DAD'S HOME COOKING

Oil (olive, peanut)

Olives (black, stuffed green)

Oysters (canned)

Pasta (egg noodles: fettuccine, lasagna, sea shells, spaghetti, elbow)

Peas (dried split)

Pineapple (canned)

Pudding mixes

Raisins

Rice (white, brown)

Salt (sea, iodized, canning and pickling)

Soups (canned)

Sugar (granulated, brown, powdered)

Tea (black, green, herbal)

Tomato (whole, diced, sauce, paste)

Tomato with Chilies (canned)

Tomato Juice (canned)

Tuna (canned)

Vegetables (canned)

Vinegar (apple cider, balsamic, white, wine)

Wheat Bran

Wine (red, white)

Worcestershire Sauce

Index

INDEX

About the Author

R. W. Owen is an architect, cook, woodworker, woodturner, gardener, and banjoist residing in Kenmore, Washington. He grew up on a farm near Hollister, Idaho and received his Bachelor of Architecture degree from the University of Idaho in 1967. His career as an architect and construction manager included serving as construction engineer for the US Pavilion Expo 74, Spokane, Washington. He retired from Lease Crutcher Lewis in 2009 after forty-two years in the construction industry. Since retiring, in addition to authoring this cookbook, he has remained active in the Puget Sound Chapter Construction Specifications Institute, and maintains his membership in the Architectural Woodwork Institute and the Seattle Chapter, American Association of Woodturners. He enjoys cooking using vegetables from his garden, making beer, wine, mustard, and pickles and entertaining dinner guests. This book contains recipes that he has prepared over the years, including for holidays and special occasions, to feed his family and guests.

Follow his cooking at: http://dadshomecookingblog.blogspot.com

Facebook: http://www.facebook.com/pages/R-W-Owen/428096413900850

Twitter: https://twitter.com/RWOwen43

Made in the USA
San Bernardino, CA
15 March 2013